The Plays Of Saunders Lewis

The Plays Of Saunders Lewis

Also translated by Joseph P. Clancy:

Volume II

HAVE A CIGARETTE?
(Gymerwch chi Sigarét? 1955)
TREASON
(Brad, 1958)
ESTHER
(1959)

in preparation:

Volume III

EXCELSIOR
(1962)
ACADEMIC AFFAIRS
(Problemau Prifysgol, 1962)
TOMORROW'S WALES
(Cymru Fydd, 1967)
ON THE TRAIN
(Yn y Trên, 1965)

Volume IV

THE DAUGHTER OF GWERN HYWEL
(Merch Gwern Hywel, 1964)
THE CONDEMNED CELL
(Cell y Grog, 1975)
THE TWO MARRIAGES OF ANN THOMAS
(Dwy Briodas Ann, 1973)

THE PLAYS OF SAUNDERS LEWIS

TRANSLATED FROM THE WELSH BY
JOSEPH P. CLANCY

VOLUME I
The Vow / *Amlyn ac Amig*
The Woman made of Flowers / *Blodeuwedd*
The King of England's Daughter / *Siwan*

Gwasg Dinefwr

'The Vow' first published 1940 in Welsh as
'Amlyn ac Amig' by Gwasg Aberystwyth
Copyright © Saunders Lewis 1940
The Translation Copyright © Joseph P. Clancy 1985

'The Woman Made of Flowers' first published 1948 in Welsh as
'Blodeuwedd' by Gwasg Gee
Copyright © Saunders Lewis 1948
The Translation Copyright © Joseph P. Clancy 1985

'The King of England's Daughter' first published 1956 in Welsh as
'Siwan' by Llyfrau'r Dryw (Christopher Davies [Publishers] Ltd.)
Copyright © Saunders Lewis 1956
The Translation Copyright ©Joseph P. Clancy 1985

Published in 1985 by
Christopher Davies (Publishers) Ltd.
Rawlings Road, Llandybie, Carmarthenshire, SA18 3YD

Published and printed in 2002 by
Dinefwr Press Ltd.
Rawlings Road, Llandybie, Carmarthenshire, SA18 3YD

ISBN 0 9540569 4 9

*All rights reserved. No part of this publication may
be reproduced, stored in a retrieval system, or
transmitted, in any form or by any means,
electronic, mechanical, photocopying, recording
or otherwise, without the prior permission of
Dinefwr Press Ltd.*

Contents

TRANSLATOR'S PREFACE	7
THE VOW	11
ACT I	13
ACT II	23
ACT III	33
THE WOMAN MADE OF FLOWERS	45
ACT I	49
ACT II	62
ACT III	75
ACT IV	84
THE KING OF ENGLAND'S DAUGHTER	99
ACT I	103
ACT II	122
ACT III	135
APPENDIX	153

Translator's Preface

Saunders Lewis (b. 1893) is, quite simply, the foremost dramatist to have written in the Welsh language. Indeed, in the absence of a strong native tradition, he may almost be said to have invented a dramatic literature for Welsh-speaking Wales, drawing eclectically upon chiefly European modes, traditional and modern, to create theatrical works of art for a culture that for much of his career had no professional theatre. The reader will find in these volumes an ample selection that shows his diversity and development as a playwright, and his continuing exploration of the conditions and consequences of choice, the tensions between *eros* and *agape*, and what William James called "the will to believe".

But these translations are intended not simply to be read, but to provide scripts for theatrical production, for the English-language audiences of Wales and elsewhere, not least my own United States. I have therefore been particularly conscious of Saunders Lewis' own statement that "audible rhythms and the music of speech are of necessity called for in the theatre", a statement which applies equally to his earlier plays in verse, the often heightened prose of his plays of the 1950s, and the more colloquial prose of the later works. I have tried in style to be both faithful to each of the original works and accessible, without excessive Americanisms, to audiences on both sides of the Atlantic. In a very few instances I have dropped or transmuted expressions or allusions incomprehensible to a Welshless audience.

The plays set in the Wales of the 1960s pose special problems, or so at least it seems to a non-Welsh translator, because of the nation's modern bi-lingualism. Must these characters be presented as speaking the English they would also use every day, or may the translator, while trying to avoid the effect of "quaintness" that has often afflicted efforts to suggest Welsh-speakers, allow them some phrasings and rhythms they would probably not carry over to their English speech? In this respect, as several readers of my typescript have noted, these translations in particular need to be tested by actors and directors. So also with my use or omission of contractions in these and the other plays: I have tended to avoid contracting when I could "hear" options I believed should be left open for the actors speaking the lines — even at the risk of having the reader occasionally find the dialogue a bit stiff. I hope indeed that all the scripts will have the benefit of more exploration in performance than I have so far been able to give them, and that whatever modifications prove useful may be incorporated in a subsequent edition.

Three of the plays were originally written for radio — two of these I have adapted for the theatre, and the third can be readily adapted by various means. One play written expressly for television had already been adapted to the stage by the playwright; a second is suited to staging without any modification. I have included, for reasons given in my prefatory notes to the work, a translation of the short novel *Merch Gwern Hywel* in Volume IV.

Prefatory notes to the plays have been chiefly designed to give a basis for programme notes rather than to offer critical analysis. I have not translated Saunders Lewis' own prefaces to various plays, since these often deal with matters of concern chiefly to Welsh-language readers at the time of the play's publication, but I have quoted from them when it seemed advisable. While I have added some information for readers when I thought it might be useful, I have been mindful that this cannot be consulted by a theatre audience and tried to keep it to a minimum.

Although I had thought in planning this book to write a full-length critical introduction, it now seems to me preferable to allow the plays to make their impact without the potential distractions of critical intervention, while giving assistance on what C. S. Lewis called "unshared backgrounds" through the prefatory notes. Readers who wish to obtain an ample view of Saunders Lewis as political theorist and activist as well as man of letters should consult *Presenting Saunders Lewis,* edited by Alun R. Jones and Gwyn Thomas, an admirable selection from his work in many genres (including earlier translations of three plays) together with critical essays on his thought and work, and the excellent monograph by Bruce Griffiths in the *Writers of Wales* series, both published by the University of Wales Press at Cardiff.

What Saunders Lewis' plays most need now, in common with much of the European, British, and American drama of the middle decades of this century, is to be regularly experienced and evaluated in the theatre, and in other countries and languages as well as in Welsh and in Wales. Although he once wrote that "the Welsh are my audience, I have sought no other", it was with Saunders Lewis' consent and encouragement that I undertook these translations, and it is my hope that they will assist in gaining for his plays a lasting international audience.

* * * *

I must thank my college, Marymount Manhattan, for the senior fellowship that allowed me to initiate this work with a stay in Cardiff during Spring 1976. For their kindness and hospitality during that time, I am grateful to Glenys and John Ormond, and to Professor Gwyn Jones and the University College of Wales, Cardiff. Professor R. M. Jones of the University College of Wales, Aberystwyth, has been warmly encouraging and shrewd in advising through the various disruptions and discouragements of these years. Patricia Falkenhain and Robert Gerringer, my ideal American Siwan and Llywelyn, have read several scripts in progress and offered professional advice, as has Diana Lawrence, my ideal American Blodeuwedd. My wife, as ever, has been a challenging and sympathetic reader, and my unfailing support and comfort.

To Saunders Lewis himself these volumes are dedicated, in tribute to a lifetime of heroic choices.

THE VOW
Amlyn ac Amig
(1940)

Amlyn ac Amig, here translated as *The Vow*, was written for radio in 1940. In his preface to the published play, which he subtitled "A Comedy", Saunders Lewis noted that it was based on a medieval tale translated from Latin into Welsh in the fifteenth century, that the original story had nothing to do with Christmas, and that whereas Amig was the focus of that story, it is the crisis and conversion of Amlyn that is central to the play. The reader may be familiar with the central characters as "Amis and Amile" — the tale belongs to "the matter of France", romances connected to the court of Charlemagne, whose daughter Amig had won for his friend by taking his place in a duel five years before the events of the drama.

The play can be readily produced for the theatre with some imaginative use of a relatively bare stage, the use of the household servants as the "choir", and perhaps the substitution of appropriate medieval carols for several of the songs. I have preferred to leave potential directors free to devise adaptations rather than to alter the script for this purpose.

CHARACTERS

Amlyn, Earl of Normandy
Belisent, his wife
Their two sons
Amig, an Earl, Amlyn's friend
Poet
Fool
Porter
Women servants
A choir

The drama takes place in a castle in Normandy, centuries ago, between Christmas Eve and Christmas Morning.

I

AMLYN: Is the door shut, porter?
PORTER: Yes, Lord Amlyn.
AMLYN: The tables are bare and there's not a sound from the kitchen.
BELISENT: A light supper tonight, my lord.
FOOL: All the meat and drink in the house
Wouldn't fill the belly of a mouse.
AMLYN: The wait is short now until midnight mass.
Gluttony is no way to prepare to greet the Christ Child.
FOOL: He put Lent before Christmas, blast the pope's eyes;
Why must we always perish to reach paradise?
BELISENT: I shall keep some food and wine ready, Amlyn,
Lest a stranger come late
And knock like Mary and Joseph on the doors of Bethlehem.
AMLYN: You are the best of wives, Belisent: your words are wise.
And you, the candles of our altar,
My two dear sons, the two eyes of your mother,
You will be up early tomorrow to praise the manger
And sing carols to Christ in the hay:
So to bed now, you rascals.
FOOL: Away with the food, away with the wine,
Away with the children and grey Advent time.
BELISENT: It is a custom, dear husband, for the children on Christmas Eve
To light a candle and place it in the window;
Since who knows if He will not come tonight as He

>
> once did to Bethlehem,
> A baby needing shelter, or in the shape of a beggar,
> And inasmuch as you do it for one of these little ones,
> You do it for Me: therefore
> These two wish before they sleep
> To light their candle to guide the mother and child through the night.
> And you, good men and women,
> Come join us in the custom:
> While the children bring their candle to gladden the way for Mary,
> Sing a Christmas carol to welcome the Mother of the Word.

(*They sing, men and women alternating couplets, but all together in the final stanza.*)

MEN:	Tell us, Mary, when you welcomed For our sake the Lord's conception?
WOMEN:	I beheld to my amazement God's own herald there before me.
MEN:	Tell us, Mary, what did Gabriel Kneeling sing of heaven's secrets?
WOMEN:	"Ave, precious vial of mercies To man's sinful generations."
MEN:	Tell us, Mary, what compelled you To accept our God within you?
WOMEN:	God has left all moments open, Never forced Himself upon us.
ALL:	Hail, O humble, ardent maiden, Wonder of the visiting angels, Maid and mother, door and wellspring, Of the Light that came among us.
AMLYN:	See, the candle has been lit. The wick is cheerful as a twinkling star. Who knows what pilgrim Seeing its flame within the weary night Will bring his blessing to you, my dear children, And to the house and household in repayment.

BELISENT:	My darlings, good night.
	Tonight the angels of the manger surround you.
	No ghosts or demon or outlandish dangers
	Will walk tonight.
	You will wake cheerfully tomorrow, the children's holiday,
	To the miracle of the birth and the smile of Christmas.
	Now ask as you go for your father's blessing.
AMLYN:	Tonight, and at the hour of death,
	The almighty Father keep you, my children, Amen.
ALL:	Good night, little lords, Merry Christmas.
AMLYN:	Do you remember, Belisent, five years ago today?
BELISENT:	How could I forget? Shall I forget Amig, our friend,
	Who risked his life for you and for me?
FOOL:	If I see him, I will give him a present.
BELISENT:	What present, Fool, have you for Amig?
FOOL:	He'll get my cap and bells, my place in the court and my flattery;
	I'm a Fool for cash; he's more of a fool voluntarily.
	Consider his case: a man risks his skin to win the emperor's daughter,
	And then gives her, with nothing to show for his pains, to his friend!
	Here's matter for laughter!
BELISENT:	But, Fool, Amig was a married man.
FOOL:	And the more of a fool not to take the pretty creature:
	Since the wife a fool gets when he ventures
	To wed's a sour she-bear who wears the trousers.
AMLYN:	Be quiet, Fool, you do not know how foolish your rhymes are.
	Not far from Paris, beside the river Seine,
	In the fields of clover,
	Is the church and abbey of Saint Germain;
	There, one afternoon, our hands on the high altar and its relics,
	We swore a vow before the Host, Amig and I —
	Never will I forget the vow ...

(A strain of music; his remembrance comes to mind with the sound of horses' hooves.)

AMIG: Here is the church. Let us go in.
You fought bravely, Amlyn.

AMLYN: You also — you almost killed me.
You know, Amig, I roamed through France to seek you.

AMIG: While I wandered through the world lamenting for Amlyn.
And then, when we came together, both of us armed like this,
Each of us thought the other a highway robber
And fought to the point of death.

AMLYN: That will not happen to us a second time.
From this hour on, should I find you in purgatory,
Or whatsoever image you may bear, Amig my friend,
My soul will leap to greet you.
Let us kneel. Let us mount to the altar.
Let us each place his hand on the relics:
I swear to God, and to you, Amig, I swear . .

AMIG: I swear to God, and to you, Amlyn, I swear . .

BOTH: That I will never fail in love or in counsel
Or anything a friend may rightly do for his friend,

AMLYN: And between us there will never be untruth.

AMIG: And between us there will never be untruth.

* * * *

AMLYN: Never will I forget the vow.

BELISENT: Oh that Amig were with us at Christmas.
What a feast and what merrymaking
There would be with the two little boys.

AMLYN: And I, if he came,
I would fill this cup of mine and his cup,
And drink deep to him.

POET: Your cup is beautiful, my lord.
Forgive the curiosity of a poet with an eye for craftsmanship;

	This is a goblet made by a goldsmith, superbly wrought of gold and silver,
	And adorned with precious stones. I have never seen its like.
AMLYN:	Nor will you for some time. You have judged shrewdly, poet.
	Pope Constantine gave it to me in Rome;
	He baptized myself and Amig together,
	Two babies brought to him in St Peter's church,
	And gave us two cups, both the same colour,
	The same size, the same goldsmith's work: seen side by side
	There is not a man living could say which is which.
POET:	And your life is the image of this cup, my lord,
	Rounded, ample,
	Without a dent or a flaw;
	Heaven has given you heaven here
	As the sun sees itself mirrored in the bosom of a lake;
	All the lands speak in praise of you,
	And your fair wife and two fine heirs;
	A precious dance through unperturbed golden hours,
	Your prosperity and children, with fortune on your side.
FOOL:	The breath of the cup's turned your head, you monkey;
	Praise is for poems; in talk it's a bogey.
BELISENT:	Let him be, Fool. Speaking the unpalatable truth belongs to you.
FOOL:	Between a poet and a fool men find out what's true.
AMLYN:	Let the poet sing, if he wishes.
POET:	I will sing the praise of the Earl of Normandy,
	And of his wife, Belisent, daughter of the Emperor of France.
FOOL:	And I, like a Fool, will bear the burden.
	(*The Poet sings, and the Company join in the refrain.*)
POET:	A tune on my harpstrings for Normandy's blessing,
	Amid boughs of holly an apple-tree praising,

	My glorious leader, his fair land's stout shield,
	The captain of joy to each town and each field.
	Here's health to our lord, our sword and our prize,
	Our source and our sunshine of life and of peace.
FOOL:	A verse to the Countess now.
POET:	My fingers now sing her gold locks, her warm laughter,
	This lily of Frenchwomen, emperor's daughter,
	Her lips are like strawberries dipped in sweet wine,
	Her smile is our springtime, our summer's bright sun.
	Here's health to our lady, the light of our feast,
	Our source and our sunshine of life and of peace.
FOOL:	And now to the children; tomorrow's feast is theirs.
POET:	My two princes' twins are the theme of my singing,
	Their beautiful nestful, bright wheat of their sowing;
	These unblemished blossoms, did earth ever bear
	Beneath a bright sky two so comely, so dear?
	Here's health to the heirs, our glory and grace,
	Our source and our sunshine of life and of peace.
	(*The sound of heavy knocking on the door*)
PORTER:	Who is this whose summons
	Beats upon the door
	And shatters the peace of the night?
	(*Knocking again*)
FOOL:	Praise be to the children, their candle has raised an early fish;
	That knocking is like the knocking of death himself.
AMLYN:	Open for him, porter. None will be turned away tonight.

(*The porter is heard opening, and just after there is the noise of a clapper such as was used by lepers.*)

BELISENT:	Blessed Mary! It is a leper's bell.
OTHERS:	Leprosy! . . . A leper! . . . God save us all!
PORTER:	What do you wish, friend?

AMIG:	Shelter and alms for one in distress.
PORTER:	This is no hospital,
	But a house full of people waiting for Christmas;
	Go half a mile further to the house of the monks.
AMIG:	The night is dreadful; beg the master of the house
	That I may rest tonight in his stable.
FOOL:	Ha, ha! "Because there was no room for him in the inn."
BELISENT:	My lord, on the night of the birth shall we turn distress from our door?
AMLYN:	But leprosy? What of the children and the household?
BELISENT:	Christ will bring no one sadness this night
	If you trust in his name.
FOOL:	And He didn't come just to bring peace, so I've heard:
	He plays pretty strange tricks sometimes with a sword.
BELISENT:	Let there be no talk of a sword tonight.
AMLYN:	What does the man look like, porter?
PORTER:	There is nobility in his voice. I did not see his face.
AMLYN:	Bring him in that I may question him,
	And let everyone stay on this side of the table.
	(*The clapping is heard approaching.*)
AMIG:	A blessing on this house and its merciful household.
AMLYN:	Where have you come from, friend, and who are you?
AMIG:	An exile from afar, under the hand and punishment of God.
POET:	Ah, his face. Do you see? It's been eaten away
	Until his mother would not recognize him.
AMLYN:	Why are you wandering like this at Christmas?
AMIG:	I have a friend — if he knew of my affliction,
	He would give me shelter and care,
	And to reach him is my aim.
AMLYN:	Have you no family to care for you?
AMIG:	I had a wife. Now I am worse than a widower.
AMLYN:	Your answers are courteous, friend,
	And though your fortune is wretched, you are not

	without breeding;
	If you wish to remain here tonight, we will give you a roof and a pillow;
	You know how wary one must be of a leper.
AMIG:	God reward you, lord;
	Here too there are tears for the things of man
	And the turns of men's fortunes touch the human heart.
BELISENT:	Do you wish some food, friend?
AMIG:	May I have a drink of wine?
BELISENT:	You may, and welcome.
AMIG:	No, my lady, not from your cup,
	Lest a maid take harm from washing it.
	I have my own cup; pour the wine into this.
BELISENT:	The cup! Oh, the cup! Holy Mary!
POET:	The same colour, same shape as the cup on the table:
	There is not a man living could say which is which.
FOOL:	The old story of Benjamin:
	If a cup's in the bag, it's clear
	A cup will come out, never fear.
AMLYN:	Stranger, leper,
	Are you a thief and a robber? Is that the cause of your punishment?
	That cup in your hand, its owner would not give it willingly.
	Do you know who it was you killed? And to whom you have come for revenge?
AMIG:	In a tournament, fairly, and for my friend,
	Only so have I taken anyone's life.
	Whether that is the cause of my punishment, I do not know.
POET:	In a tournament? Ah God, was he once a knight?
AMLYN:	Answer me man, do not prolong my anxiety,
	How did you come to possess that cup?
AMIG:	Pope Constantine gave it to me in Rome.
AMLYN:	Amig? No, not Amig?
AMIG:	Do not touch me, Amlyn. Stay over there.
AMLYN:	Forgive my blindness. Amig, my brother.

AMIG: It is for you to forgive my coming to you so stricken,
                An ugly leper beneath your roof.
BELISENT: Let there be no talk of forgiveness. Your coming, Amig,
                Is Christmas to our hearth and home.
AMIG: It was you, Belisent, first recognized me.
BELISENT: In pouring the wine,
                For fear of the cup I gazed into your eyes.
                The leprosy that has eaten your flesh has not darkened the candles of your mind;
                In them glowed the flame of serenity I saw at the tournament of Paris.
                But I stood mute, the anguish like an arrow in my throat.
                Amig, how is it with you?
AMIG: Like a ship when the whirlwind is at its height,
                Shaken like a bone, stripped bare and white.
BELISENT: You have rowed your vessel to its harbour tonight;
                Here you will have the peace and the care of a home,
                Hands to ease your suffering, the laughter of children —
AMIG: Have you children? Praise God for that.
BELISENT: Two three-year-old boys. You will hear them tomorrow
                Calling you for Christmas.
                It was their candle led you here now.
AMLYN: Fair Belisent, let us question him no further.
                Look, his head is bent with weariness and pain.
                Tomorrow you can trace your journey, my brother,
                And the twists of fortune on the harsh road you have travelled;
                But tonight it is better to rest.
                Let us prepare for him a royal bed in my chamber.
                And you, Belisent, and the household, go all to the midnight mass
                To speak your thanks to the Child on his altar.
                As for me, I will stay to wait upon my friend,
                And at dawn we will go to church together

	To renew the vow that was made at St Germain's
	That I will never fail in love or in counsel
	Or anything a friend may rightly do for his friend —
AMIG:	And between us there will never be untruth.
AMLYN:	Never will I forget the vow.

(Music. A choir sings:)
Why so brightly shining, stars,
As if light were only yours?
Christus natus hodie,
Light itself is born as God and man.
The waves are chanting melody,
Soft breeze sings him lullaby,
Ex Maria Virgine,
For heaven's babe who lies in Bethlehem town.

Noel. Noel. Noel. Noel.
At the stroke of starry midnight,
Softly, not a cry or birth-pang,
Jesus, pearl of heaven, slipped from Mary's womb.
Noel. Noel.

Angels of the heavenly choirs,
What great wonder now is ours?
Ecce qui creavit nos
A psalm fills heaven, come for our salvation.
Israel, now be at peace,
Here your years of suffering cease,
Lux fulgebit super vos,
And dawn like dew refreshes all creation.

Noel. Noel. Noel. Noel.
At the stroke of starry midnight,
Softly, not a cry or birth-pang,
Jesus, pearl of heaven, slipped from Mary's womb.
Noel. Noel.

II

THE ARCHANGEL
RAPHAEL: Amig, are you sleeping?
AMIG: No, friend Amlyn.
RAPHAEL: You have answered rightly. It is a friend calls you,
But I am not Amlyn.
AMIG: Who are you, Lord?
And how have you come to me like this in the middle of the night?
RAPHAEL: I am an angel of God named Raphael.
AMIG: From the depth of my emptiness
Welcome, my lord Archangel,
If you come to claim my soul.
RAPHAEL: No, my friend, death does not desire his prey.
You have made yourself loved by the angels of heaven
Who sang praise to God seeing you in your sorrow
With uncomplaining voice like Job;
The Lord has sent me, this night,
To his saint to heal him.
AMIG: How shall I be healed, Lord?
God's will be done. But I tremble, I am fearful.
Lead me not, weak as I am, into tribulation,
But save me from evil.
RAPHAEL: Amlyn your friend has two small sons;
Ask him to kill them with his sword, and then
Wash you from head to foot with their blood.
Thus, says God, your body will be healed.
AMIG: Angel Raphael, God does not ask this?
RAPHAEL: I am a messenger, Amig. His is the way.
AMIG: Ask my only friend

	To kill his two children with his own hand
	To rid me of pain?
RAPHAEL:	I did not say that. It is not to mend the body
	He sends archangels to a world steeped in blasphemy.
	But on a more important way He went himself, a poor baby,
	On a journey to Gethsemane from the straw of the stable.
AMIG:	This will be, then, for the good of Amlyn's soul?
RAPHAEL:	It is easier for a camel to pass through the eye of a needle
	Than for a rich man to enter the kingdom of heaven.
AMIG:	My lord Archangel, to me once was given
	The privilege of risking my body for his.
	Listen now to my entreaty:
	If his life is too much at ease,
	And his prayers go to heaven over his shoulder,
	And he is too firmly attached to his wife and his sons,
	If, on feast days, he is more than likely to sin
	By mouthing conventional pieties to God,
	Let the price of his pardon fall on me:
	Deepen my plague, let your hand be heavier upon me,
	Put me once more, an outcast, to flight
	And for his sake accept all my sufferings.
RAPHAEL:	It is sweet and seemly to suffer
	For the needs of a dear friend;
	But if it is God who fixes sorrow on his children
	Their woeful laments will be turned to glory.
	There is only
	One wound that would forever be dreadful,
	Not to be one of the saints.
	Is this what you desire for Amlyn?
AMLYN:	*(from his bed)* Amig, Amig. Who is here?
AMIG:	There is no one here, my friend.
AMLYN:	I woke up. I heard voices conversing.

AMIG: I was saying my prayers.
Forgive me for waking you.
AMLYN: No, there is someone with you in the room . . .
Is the door open?
(He is heard crossing the room in the darkness.)
No. The door is shut.
(Approaching Amig's bed)
Amig, who was with you?
AMIG: There was no living man, my friend,
Only myself praying and pleading to God.
AMLYN: I sensed him. Someone else, not you.
I will swear that he mentioned my name.
AMIG: *(excitedly)* How? What did you hear?
AMLYN: Ha, you have had a fright. So there was someone here.
AMIG: Your name is on my lips more often than anyone's name
But intercessions are proper only for heaven's ear.
AMLYN: It was not you that named me. It was another's voice.
AMIG: I have said, my friend: no living man was here.
AMLYN: Why are you frightened, Amig? Where is your usual courage?
If a serving-lad or an escort was with you, as would fit your former station,
What is the good of hiding them, or sending them away by night?
There is freedom here for your servants as there is for me and my household,
And it will be Belisent's privilege to feed them.
AMIG: *(laughing)* My escort is snug beneath your roof.
My only servant is the leprosy that clings to me faithfully.
Go to your bed, my lord, and sleep, for Christmas has come.
AMLYN: No, on my oath.
I know that a stranger entered this house and this room of mine.

	My most faithful friend, do not abuse my welcome any longer.
	For the love that has been between us, for the tenderness of Belisent my wife
	Who prepared with her own hands this royal bed,
	Tell me: who was conversing here?
AMIG:	Have I not said no living man was here?
AMLYN:	Then what was here?
AMIG:	Do not ask me, Amlyn, for the love of God.
	Do not ask me.
AMLYN:	I have a right to know.
AMIG:	It is heaven for you that you do not know.
AMLYN:	I must know.
AMIG:	There is nothing harder for me than to tell you.
	Because, by telling it,
	I know I would never have your love and your fellowship
	Ever, ever thereafter.
AMLYN:	I swear my oath to God,
	Whatever you say, I will never be angry with you.
AMIG:	You cannot promise that. You do not know, you do not imagine
	The pit that will open between us if I speak.
AMLYN:	Do you doubt the word I have given?
AMIG:	It was Raphael the archangel came to me from God.
	(A moment's pause)
AMLYN:	It is not so strange. Your conversations
	Have been among heaven's angels for some time.
	What does the angel desire of me?
AMIG:	Why of you? Why will you rush into the lake of misery?
	It was to me the angel gave his command.
	Let the punishment for my disobedience fall on me.
AMLYN:	His message was for me. I have a right to know it.
AMIG:	Everyone has a right to his pain. A person has no other right.
	But to give a man his right, it is the grace of God can do that.
	Amlyn, do not ask of me your right.

	Do not ask further.
AMLYN	I have given my word. You must confess.
	If the message is God's, God cannot promise evil.
AMIG:	Here are his words:
	Amlyn your friend has two small sons;
	Ask him to kill them with his sword, and then
	Wash you from head to foot with the blood.
	Thus, says God, your body will be healed.
	(After a moment of silence, Amlyn breaks into unnatural laughter.)
AMLYN:	I deserve this. You caught me fairly, like an insect in a trap.
	But, friend, your drollery tonight is bitter.
	Is it your leprosy has made you so unnatural?
AMIG:	Go to bed, my lord. The game is over now.
	I am free, and you. Tomorrow, I will set out once more.
AMLYN:	Free, how?
AMIG:	From your command and from the angel's request.
AMLYN:	Was the angel's request to prepare two coffins for my children
	To set the Christmas table for me and their mother?
	Archangels are peculiar creatures.
AMIG:	Yes, disrespectful like all petitioners.
AMLYN:	And their names are Lying and Envy.
	When you came here, Amig, you were welcomed with joy;
	A leper and a homeless outcast, you found honour and respect and love.
	You saw the sunshine of my house and the dawn of Belisent,
	You heard of my two sons, the two heirs of my power,
	The goad of the gods to men that stirs them to excellence,
	To establish the glory of a line from father to son to grandson.
	Childless yourself, you saw this and in your weakness

	You were consumed by the poison of envy and blind malice.
	You tossed here in your bed, you planned a revenge
	To take on me, at Christmas, a blizzard and winter of ruin.
	The leprosy has made you cruel, Amig, to repay good with evil like this.
AMIG:	My lord, it was not as if with news of great joy I rushed to tell my story,
	And it was not without compulsion I revealed it.
AMLYN:	I did not know it was jealousy festered within you.
AMIG:	I did not invent the angel whose voice you swore you heard.
AMLYN:	But you willed the brutal slaughter of his message.
AMIG:	In God's name, may you not be right.
AMLYN:	Are you not afraid to attribute to God the cruelty of Herod?
AMIG:	What I am is a wretch who fears the face of man More than faceless God.
AMLYN:	Why then were you not frightened of your angel?
AMIG:	Because at first it was my death I welcomed.
AMLYN:	How do you know it was an angel?
AMIG:	He said so.
AMLYN:	Did you see him?
AMIG:	No, I only heard his voice.
AMLYN:	What sort of voice has an archangel That you would recognize it?
AMIG:	You heard it, Amlyn.
AMLYN:	It was a man's voice I heard, a man's voice uttering my name.
AMIG:	It was a man's voice that called me, a voice like your voice.
AMLYN:	Would an angel be as unremarkable as that?
AMIG:	Was it not as a man that the Son of Man came to men?
	We can only hear an angel as a man.
AMLYN:	Have you ever before heard the speech of an angel?
AMIG:	Never.

AMLYN: Can you prove to me that it was Raphael?
AMIG: How can I? Neither could Joseph
When he heard in a dream, "Do not fear to wed Mary."
AMLYN: Tell me, Amig, if it came into the Devil's mind
To tempt you that he might damn a hated soul
And drive him to curse God,
Would he not speak with the voice of a man?
AMIG: Heaven preserve me from that.
AMLYN: Answer me. Would it not be with a voice like your friend's
That a Devil would call your name in the darkness?
AMIG: Yes, that is how he would call.
AMLYN: What do you suppose? Would he shout in your ear
That he was the snarer of your soul?
AMIG: No. It is not in his own shape a demon appears.
AMLYN: Would it not be rather as a heavenly archangel
Bringing you a charge to test the faith of your friend
That a Devil would rouse the secret longing of your heart
As a horrible summons of God in the night?
AMIG: Who knows? The heart is deceitful above all things
And desperately wicked. Who can know it?
AMLYN: Will you swear to me it was an angel?
AMIG: No, because I do not know. But I will say I believe
That he was Raphael, and depend upon God
Not to leave me prey to the Devil.
To walk like one who sees, while knowing the night of the blind,
Is the daily life of faith.
God asks of you also only to judge according to your light,
And if for fear of devils or the malice of my heart
You judge my message false, then your spirit will be calm,
Putting the nightmare of tonight from your mind.
When the dawn comes I too will go yonder to the church,

	Through the leper's window I will follow the Christmas mass,
	And I will leave my blessing on you and your household forever.
AMLYN:	Amig, I am a man of flesh and blood,
	Quick-tempered, wild in my passions, as you remember of old.
	But I will fight for my children now,
	The children who are dearer to me than my own life;
	They have lain on my bosom a hundred times, here in my arms, —
	I could not, I cannot kill them.
AMIG:	I could not either, Amlyn. Enough pain has been laid upon you.
	I argued with the angel only to avoid
	The brief anguish of this talk. And I supposed in my passion
	It was for you I pleaded; thus in my prayer to God
	Is a man's heart deceived.
	And you, you have done what you could. God's way, man does not understand it.
	Go to your bed now, my friend.
AMLYN:	To my bed? How could I rest?
	You have sprinkled a poison on my pillow that devoured sleep.
	O that I were an angel or else a devil.
	To slip into the covert of your soul and snatch the true or the false.
	If what you said tonight is true, malice on the throne of creation
	Plays with the fools of men like a cat passing sentence on a barn;
	If a lie is within your breast, what further life will be mine
	When half of my soul, — my witness that baptism's honest —
	Nurses the pus of his madness in a festering heart?
	Tonight, this Christmas night, to me the world has turned to dung,

	I have filled my barns with the sacks of its smoke.
	Yes, sooner would I kill my children than embitter them with the mention of my friend.
AMIG:	There is only One true friend.
AMLYN:	Amig, the night is too black for me to see your face or your eyes;
	Here in the dark you too are only a voice like an angel,
	Only a voice like death.
	A long time ago there was a man I called friend,
	He bore the same name as you;
	On the relics of a saint, on the altar of the sacrament,
	He gave his word to God and his word to me;
	My lord Amig,
	Do you remember the vow sworn at Saint Germain?
AMIG:	"Let us kneel. Let us mount to the altar;
	Let us each lay his hand on the relics."
	I swear to God, and to you, Amlyn, I swear —
AMLYN:	I swear to God, and to you, Amig, I swear —
BOTH:	That I will never fail in love or in counsel
	Or anything a friend may rightly — may rightly — do for his friend —
AMIG:	"And between us there will never be untruth."
AMLYN:	I determine your fate by the vow,
	And as your soul may be saved,
	Is it true he that came to you
	Said as you say?
AMIG:	As my soul may be saved,
	True, my lord, too true.
AMLYN:	*(retreating to his bed)*
	Never will I forget the vow.

*   *   *   *

The choir sings:

    Silent night, holy night,
    On the rooftop, shining bright,
    Snow like rose leaves; in the hay

Mary on her knees to pray:
There in a manger is God.

Silent night, holy night,
Lake and ditch calm and white;
Love holds the hour; near the hill
Early lambs are silent, still:
The Lamb of God has been born.

III

FIRST
SERVANT GIRL: Good morning, Porter.
SECOND
SERVANT GIRL: Merry Christmas to you, Porter.
PORTER: Good afternoon, wenches.
FIRST GIRL: Listen to the old nitpicker taunting us
Because he was up a quarter of an hour before us.
SECOND GIRL: And when all of us were at the midnight mass.
And it isn't light yet.
PORTER: Make haste, girls, to set the table;
Fetch the cups and the flagons;
The household will be thirsty when they return.
SECOND GIRL: What's it like outside, porter? Let me see.
The mist is rising from the meadow. I can see as far
as the church door.
FIRST GIRL: I wonder if Amlyn went to the early mass?
The door of his room is shut.
PORTER: I saw the leper making his way there,
Like a thorn-bush walking.
SECOND GIRL: The countess was with us at midnight.
FIRST GIRL: She didn't sleep long. She went back to the early
mass.
I'll take communion at the children's mass, she said.
PORTER: There are people coming out of the church.
Pile the fire into a bonfire to greet them.
What's come over them — dancing and caroling?
SECOND GIRL: Let me see. Ha, ha. Like drunkards, with their
hands round each other's necks,
And their legs are so funny, out of sight in the mist.
Christmas has come, tra, la, la.
Dance with me, porter, and I'll give you a kiss.

PORTER:	I'd rather have a box on the ear. It would hurt less.
FIRST GIRL:	Here is Earl Amlyn... Merry Christmas, my lord. The children are not up yet.
AMLYN:	No? Let them sleep. It is still early.
FIRST GIRL:	There'll be high old complaining when they see everyone down. Their candle has burnt itself out.
PORTER:	There's a strange merriment at the door of the church, my lord.
FIRST GIRL:	My lord is shivering with the cold. Stand by the fire, sir. Will you take some wine to warm you?
PORTER:	Something is afoot, my lord. There's the Fool dancing his way here.
SECOND GIRL:	Let me see, you fat thing.
PORTER:	The countess is following, and the household.
SECOND GIRL:	There's a strange knight walking with the countess. A tall one, handsome and slender.
FIRST GIRL:	Where has the leper gone, I wonder?
AMLYN:	Has he left?
PORTER:	He went to the mass, my lord.
AMLYN:	Look and see if he is returning with the household.
SECOND GIRL:	Let me see. No, he isn't, my lord.
AMLYN:	That is good.
FIRST GIRL:	May I wake the children to greet their mother, my lord? There is only an hour before the last mass.
AMLYN:	Let them sleep on. It will be hard enough to wake them.
PORTER:	The countess is walking on the arm of the strange knight. If you were not by the fire, my lord, I would swear he was Amlyn.
FOOL:	*(from far off)* Oyez! Oyez! Oyez!
FIRST GIRL:	You are still cold, my lord. Here is a cup of wine.
AMLYN:	Leave it. I do not wish to drink.
FIRST GIRL:	You are going to communion then? I don't believe you should.

	Your fingers are dead white.
AMLYN:	They were red enough earlier. Two hands, two corpses.
BELISENT:	Pull me along with you, Amig.
	My feet will not keep up with my desire.
	It is true, isn't it? You are you? Say it is so.
AMIG:	I myself, Belisent.
BELISENT:	Come, let's run together again.
	It's folly to be a woman's escort.
	I'm laughing and weeping by turns, and forever tripping while running.
	Make haste to Amlyn, make haste.
PORTER:	There's been an odd communion at the church.
	That whole congregation is drunk.
SECOND GIRL:	Let me see, let me see. I don't know why, but I'm reeling already too.
FOOL:	*(closer)* Oyez! Oyez! Oyez!
FIRST GIRL:	It's high time I got the children up to see the merriment.
	Does the earl have a fever, would you say? Did he touch the leper?
BELISENT:	Let us walk again, Amig. I am out of breath dancing.
	Yesterday you were crippled and sick, and today you're like a lad.
FOOL:	*(having arrived)*
	Oyez! Oyez! Good news for Christmas.
PORTER:	What's all the commotion?
FOOL:	Am I not telling you? A wonder! A miracle!
SECOND GIRL:	Let me see, let me see. What is going on, Fool?
FOOL:	Haven't I told you already? Let a man catch his breath.
SECOND GIRL:	What did you say? What is it?
FOOL:	I've said it over and over. Why won't you believe it, you dolts?
PORTER:	It is Christmas today. It will be New Year's a week from today.
	That's the Fool's wonder.
	He has lost his breath running here to tell it.

POET:	*(having arrived)*
	Has the earl heard? Where is he?
FIRST GIRL:	Over by the fire. Go to him, poet, so we can hear the story.
POET:	My lord, have you heard the news?
FOOL:	Of Amig, Amlyn, of Amig,
	Who has made all of us stutter.
POET:	Who is now like your twin brother.
FOOL:	No wonder he took your place in the tournament of Paris.
POET:	Your two gold cups are not more like each other.
FOOL:	More easily stolen, though.
AMLYN:	What is all this? Did everyone go out of his mind like me,
	And lose his senses last night?
FOOL:	Amig's lost his leprosy,
	I have lost my wind;
	That's quite enough to lose, I'd say,
	Without your loss of mind.
SECOND GIRL:	Here they are. See the countess on Amig's arm.
	Come here, porter, I must give a kiss to something.
PORTER:	There's the door. That's as wide as your mouth.
	Countess, my lord.
BELISENT:	O Amlyn, the short way from the church was all too long
	So great was the weight of my joy.
	Heaven has given us a Christmas gift:
	Behold Amig, your friend, in good health.
ALL sing:	Sun and moon and stars, rejoice now,
	Sing praise to God;
	Waters of the skies, give voice now,
	Sing praise to God;
	Frost and snow and dew and shower,
	Ocean winds, and summer, winter,
	Lightning, thunder, sing hosanna,
	Sing praise to God.
BELISENT:	Let us all drink to Amig, health and long happiness.
THE COMPANY:	To Amig . . . A blessed Christmas to Amig.

POET:	He was taken from agony, death's grip;
	Our weeping ceases to be —
FOOL:	Let his sores and leprosy
	Live with tapeworm, louse, and flea.
BELISENT:	You are not drinking, dear Amlyn. Are you going to the last communion?
AMLYN:	I have given God sufficient sacrifice.
	He will not ask more of me.
	Is this Amig or a phantom?
BELISENT:	Husband, why do you doubt?
AMLYN:	How was he restored to health?
BELISENT:	Still was the household congregation on our knees in the gloom of the church,
	Intent as the two candles that were lit on the altar stone,
	And the Light of the world in the centre concentrated our hearts
	On the arms of the candlestick of his cross.
	The low mass, sweet daily worship,
	Sanctified with its familiarity the birthday of the Word.
	Outside in the mist was Amig, bending through the leper's window,
	Excommunicate from the choir,
	But he was snatched on the wings of our prayer and the hands of a pure angel
	With the Sacrifice into the presence of the Lord.
	Intense was the joy of communion.
	The fervent doves of the parish at the table of the seraphim
	Opened wide their beaks to swallow the heavenly grain;
	And when I saw Amig in the circle there, I was not surprised or disturbed,
	For right long has he been holy, with angels his companions —
AMLYN:	May the Devil choke you, woman.
BELISENT:	Dear Amlyn, what is this?
AMLYN:	Nothing, nothing.

	I have had enough for a while of talk about angels.
	I have not yet heard when the knight was healed.
BELISENT:	You tell that, Amig.
AMIG:	I was leaning on the leper's window
	Like one in Hades peering at an opening in heaven,
	And I heard a voice calling me —
AMLYN:	A voice? Again a voice? Persistently you pile up lies.
	You know it was not a voice that healed you.
BELISENT:	My lord husband, you are like someone completely out of his mind.
	Always the grace of Christmas is the summons of heaven's messengers;
	They came to Mary, and to the wise men from the east;
	They sang to the fields of shepherds;
	And they are near us now.
	From the time the children lighted their flame in the window last night
	And the door was opened to welcome Christ in the crippled leper,
	A rustling of wings around us
	Fashioned miracles of grace.
	A Christmas gift from heaven is Amig's health.
AMLYN:	Heaven is not a giver but a bargainer,
	And bitter are its dealings.
BELISENT:	O Amlyn, do not curse today.
	I know what is causing your bitterness.
	The children who sweeten Christmas are still sleeping,
	And empty would be the feast of the Birth and the miracle of our friend's recovery
	Without the laughter and chatter of those two.
	I will go wake them quickly.
AMLYN:	Woman, behold my sword.
	I will thrust it into your heart if you go near the children.
BELISENT:	God help you, husband.
	There is blood on your sword.

AMLYN:	Two doves I killed earlier; innocents who did not flee from me.
	That is nothing. Guard your own throat.
AMIG:	Belisent, do not be disturbed. What troubles your lord
	Is a father's anxiety for his sons and his fear of a dreadful punishment.
	But, Amlyn, the unwrathful God, He has exceeded our merits;
	He proved last night we are insects in ease and adversity;
	He burdened us to the utmost power of a man to suffer.
	Today he has forgiven unworthiness, forgiven me my promise,
	He has turned away my uncleanness as a mark of his great mercy.
	The trial has passed, my lord, and so too your sacrifice.
	And the dawn has come. Go to the children; do not be afraid.
BELISENT:	What is all this, my lords?
AMLYN:	Tell her, Amig, and the price that was put on your health.
AMIG:	Last night, when all was in tranquil silence
	And night at midpoint of its rapid course,
	A voice came to me, Countess, like a furious warrior,
	And filled the room with death.
AMLYN:	A voice, only a voice.
	A tongue saying a thing, like a man in his right mind,
	Parts of speech conjoined,
	Uttering sentences,
	And behold, water will be wine, or bread flesh,
	Or two persons one flesh,
	At the explosion of the words.
	From a changeless word,

| | From an arrow that left the bowstring.
| | And for me last night there was meaning and order
| | in life,
| | As in the multitude of bits of glass
| | That figure in a church window an image of
| | paradise;
| | And a word came to my friend,
| | A voice in the night speaking and then falling silent,
| | And behold the window of reason is in pieces
| | beneath my feet
| | And life is filth.
BELISENT: At what hour was this?
AMIG: At midnight.
BELISENT: The hour of the angels of the manger.
What did your voice say?
AMIG: "Amlyn, your friend, has two small sons;
Ask him to kill them with his sword, and then
Wash you from head to foot with their blood:
Thus, says God, will your body be healed."
BELISENT: *(weakly)* Yes . . . What happened then?
AMIG: Tears streaming and suspicions,
Leave-taking and accusations;
Ice, where two hearts had been;
Then this miracle at dawn.
AMLYN: You slept afterwards, Amig?
AMIG: My weariness overcame me.
AMLYN: I never saw better sleeping —
Like the sleep of a corpse washed for its burial.
AMIG: Forgive me, Amlyn.
AMLYN: What need of forgiveness? Sleep was proper for you.
It was I, not you, was asked to kill his sons.
Was your heavy sleep not lucky as blood was poured
    into the sores,
And the foul carcass was tossed and turned to wash
    it from head to toe?
BELISENT: My love, you have been in the torments of Hell.
I will go fetch the children.
You will see that heaven does not take vengeance on
    the powerlessness of man.

AMLYN: Slowly. My sword is still unsheathed.
You approach on peril of your life.
You slept heavily, my friend, —
Through the prayerless hours unbroken by the voice of a single angel —
BELISENT: The hours of the shepherds and the Child —
AMLYN: The hours of the murderer's nightmares.
Under the iron of their black nails I argued that God would not require slaughter,
That reason and law and necessity were a shield for my children in the night.
But when this knight called on the vow that I swore as a knight —
AMIG: You frighten me, Amlyn. I never called on it.
AMLYN: You knew when our argument was ended the vow was like a glove in front of me.
Listen to me a moment: I did not believe in your angel:
I believe now and I shiver in my lost soul.
Last night when I heard you were asleep,
I rose through the gloom to gaze on your perjured sleeping.
If you feared the death of my house, would you not escape to the darkness,
Not lie there peacefully in the gutter of my pain?
I looked at your shape of sickness — it would have been easy for me to smother you,
But the peace of your sleep stood like stubborn watchmen around you.
Not because I believed your word or the chirp of prayer,
Not for the honour of a celebrated friendship,
Not out of obedience to your angel,
Did I walk the way that was before me.
But only because a vow held me, the vow of a knight with his hand on the relics,
Held me bound to my fate, yes, were heaven untrue,
Because of that, without God, without faith, or hope, or love,

	I drew my sword from the sheath.

        I drew my sword from the sheath.
        My lady and the mother of my children,
        You whom I have rendered so miserable,
        Brief will be my leave-taking.
        The hour has come for me to flee from your presence as a vagabond in disgrace;
        And when my shadow is seen hereafter, mothers will put their fingers on their lips
        And the suckling child will be silent without the breast being bared.
        Know then and understand: under the curse of the judgement
        I raised the sword in my right hand, I challenged Raphael to stop me,
        I delayed for a cold minute without a voice or a sign, nothing:
        And the sword fell.

AMIG: You killed the children?

AMLYN: *(as if to himself now)*
        Two slender bodies will be buried today,
        Frail ones who loved me;
        Woe to my hand that struck them . . .
        Two slender bodies will be buried today,
        Bones of my bones;
        My sword pierced them, these two.
        God, in his hatred, will not bury me too.

BELISENT: Clear the tables, women.
        Prepare two biers there.
        I will go fetch the children.
        (The bells of the Church toll slowly, while the poet sings.)

POET: *(singing low)* What the echoing
        Cry heard in Rama,
        Sobbing, lamenting,
            Gnashing of teeth?
        Fierce is her keening,
            Bethlehem of Judah,
        Rachel bewailing
            Her children's death.

Multitude sounding
>Hymns of His praises,
Lamb's mighty torrents,
>Innocents slain,
Hundreds of thousands
>Robed in your radiance,
Gospel's first harvest,
>Hear now our pain.

Jesus we beg you,
>*Kyrie eleison,*
For consolation
>In our distress.
We who confess to,
>*Christe eleison,*
Spurning so often
>Your graciousness.

(Suddenly through the knell of the bells, joyful caroling; one hears the laughter of the two children approaching, and then their voices calling:)

CHILDREN: Merry Christmas, Mama.
Dada, may we go to the manger now?

BELISENT: Behold me, and the children the Lord has given me
As signs and wonders.
I found them playing in bed.
See the small red strips like gold ribbons around their necks
Where the sword struck . . .
Do not stand there, my dears, lest you frighten the babies;
They know of nothing but sleep beneath the wings of guardian angels.
It is the Saviour's constant mercy has done all this.

AMIG: In dust and ashes will I kneel,
Since my eyes have seen Your salvation.

AMLYN: My eyes have beheld the Lord;
And I am loathsome to myself.

O Amig, Mary's Child was born without a cry or a pang;
But a pang worse than death was his birth within my heart.
I have never before seen these boys;
It was my own pride I fondled, the continuation and promise of my life,
The vigour and strength of my seed and the splendour of the loins of my wife;
I loved my self in them more than I loved my own life;
And I was killed in them by God with my own hand.
Now they are God's, not mine.
And it is God in them I worship;
The child Jesus has turned every child henceforth to a sacrament.
Come, Belisent and Amig, let us follow the chldren to the manger
And lay them at the Virgin's feet as gold, frankincense, and myrrh.

(And the choir sings the Latin carol, "Adeste fideles", as they go to the manger.)

THE WOMAN MADE OF FLOWERS

Blodeuwedd
(1947)

In his foreword to *Blodeuwedd* in 1948, Saunders Lewis remarked somewhat wryly that "it would be a help to understanding the characters if the Welsh audience were as familiar with the *Mabinogi* as a Greek audience was with their ancient stories." For a non-Welsh audience, in particular, some prior knowledlge of the medieval tale "Math Son of Mathonwy", on which the play is based, seems essential. The following summary of the incidents in the story that have a bearing on the play is offered as an aid to the reader and a basis for programme notes. The complete tale may be read in any of the several available translations of *The Mabinogion*; I have used that by Gwyn Jones and Thomas Jones for quotations.

Arianrhod was the niece of Math, ruler of the realm of Gwynedd in North Wales. She was compelled to prove her claim to virginity by stepping over a magic wand; when a male child dropped from her womb, Arianrhod fled from Math's court in disgrace.

The boy was raised by Arianrhod's brother Gwydion, a magician. When Gwydion brought him, still nameless, to Arianrhod's castle, she "swore a destiny on him" that he should never have a name unless he received it from her. On the following day Gwydion used his magic to disguise himself and the boy as shoemakers and arrived in a boat before Arianrhod's castle. The quality of their shoes was such that she was lured down to the boat so that her foot could be measured properly. While Gwydion was doing this, a wren alighted on the boat, and the boy aimed at it with his cobbler's needle and hit it "between the sinew of its leg and the bone". Arianrhod exclaimed: "With a deft hand the fair one hit it." Gwydion replied: "He has now got a name, and good enough is his name. Lleu Llaw Gyffes (deft-handed fair one) is he from now on."

But when Gwydion lifted the spell and Arianrhod recognized her brother and her son, she swore another destiny on the boy, that he would never bear arms until she herself equipped him. Gwydion, by a further use of his magical powers, arranged a situation in which Arianrhod, believing her fortress to be under attack, gladly armed her disguised son.

But when the spell was lifted, and she found that her second curse had been thwarted, Arianrhod swore still a third destiny on her son, "that he shall never gain a wife of the race that is now on this earth." Gwydion went to Math, and Math suggested that they "conjure a wife for him out of flowers". And so "they took the flowers of the oak, and the flowers of the broom, and the flowers of the meadow-sweet, and from those they called forth the very fairest and best endowed maiden that mortal ever saw . . . and named her Blodeuedd (flowers)." After that Math bestowed the lordship of the district of Ardudwy on Lleu. It is at this point in the story that the play begins.

Saunders Lewis employs later versions of two names for stronger poetic effect. "Lleu" becomes "Llew", which means "lion": the frequent play on words thus achieved is inevitably lost in translation. "Blodeuedd" becomes "Blodeuwedd", which means "flower features".

The play assumes knowledge of an earlier portion of the tale which can be briefly summarized. Gwydion's brother Gilfaethwy lusted after a maiden at Math's court, and Gwydion so managed things that Gilfaethwy was able to rape the girl. Math punished his nephews for this by turning the brothers first into a hind and a stag, next into a boar and a sow, and lastly into male and female wolves. Each of these transformations lasted for a year, and each resulted in offspring. Math then relented, saying: "Great shame have you had, that each one of you has had young by the other."

A few other references in the play need annotation. Annwn is the Other World or fairyland of Celtic myth, and its chief dwelling-place is Caer Siddi. Pryderi was ruler of Dyfed in South Wales in these stories.

DRAMATIS PERSONAE

Blodeuwedd
Llew Llaw Gyffes
Gwydion
Gronw Pebr
Rhagnell
The Captain of Penllyn's Household Guard
Soldiers and Servants

ACT I

(A castle in Ardudwy. Gwydion and Llew Llaw Gyffes)

LLEW:	*(clapping his hands)* Ho, one of you, come here . . . *(A servant enters)* Are the horses ready?
SERVANT:	The horses and the men, sir, all are ready. And the arms of gold and the silk brocade, your gifts.
LLEW:	Where is my lady?
SERVANT:	In her chamber, sir, Embroidering, she and her maids, and listening To the bard harping.
LLEW:	Go to her, inform her Today we travel three hours until sundown, Gwydion and myself and the soldiers with us; She is to come at once to bid us goodbye.
SERVANT:	Yes, my lord. *(He goes)*
LLEW:	O, uncle, foster-father, No man in Gwynedd is as wretched as I.
GWYDION:	Tush, tush. Compose yourself. No more moaning.
LLEW:	I am the most miserable man on earth; My mother's hate and her curses have harried me From the womb to this day, hatred and rage and doom.
GWYDION:	*You* can say this, who have enjoyed the greatest friendship ever known? You, a by-blow flung on the doorsill scarcely breathing, and weaker than a chick just out of the shell? You, after you had three of the most dreadful fates in the world laid upon you, and I

	thwarted them all, giving you a name, and arms, and the most marvellous woman created and the finest domain in Earth's own kingdom? Shame on you.
LLEW:	No one ever had a better friend than you, Gwydion.
GWYDION:	No, and no one else the trouble I have had with friends. There was my brother, Gilfaethwy: I lived for years with the wild beasts on his account, not knowing my place in the world, male and female in turn, and the brood I had better left unmentioned. And then there is you, and who knows what harm will befall me because of you, when your own mother is bent on destroying you if I did not thwart her.
LLEW:	And a mother's vengeance is stronger than your love.
GWYDION:	How so? Her schemes have been demolished, haven't they? When she refused to give you a name, I saw to it you were named. She laid a doom upon you that you would never gain arms: I saw to it you were armed by her own hands. She doomed you never to find a wife among the daughters of men: I fashioned for you out of flowers the loveliest maiden that eyes have seen.
LLEW:	And yet, I have not escaped my mother's rage — Blodeuwedd is not at all like other women.
GWYDION:	To be sure. I am old and incredibly experienced, and in my time I have loved many women and wild beasts, but never in my life have I seen a woman who was like other women.
LLEW:	Gwydion, listen to me, she has no children.
GWYDION:	You are lucky. The last child I had — he was a wolf.
LLEW:	Never, I will never forget the daybreak When I saw for the very first time Blodeuwedd; Yourself and Math came walking across the glade, And between you, naked as the blossoms of dawn, The dew undried upon her cold breasts, Breasts as pure as a lily's heart when night Holds it to her bosom, there she walked, The virgin spring's soul embodied in flesh.

	I looked at her, and she in turn at me,
	And I clothed her nakedness with burning kisses;
	And these arms, the lusty arms of youth —
	My arms so long empty — her cincture of steel.
GWYDION:	The old story. I have embraced all sorts of females.
	And believe me, boy, on a spring morning, the
	softest girl's flesh and a boar's bristles are much the
	same.
LLEW:	But she was cold, Lord Gwydion, cold.
	My heart, that was throbbing on her breast,
	Broke like glass on flint. I have never seen
	Warmth in her face, only the beauty of a moon
	Dawning indifferently above the world.
	Her blood is strange and alien. One night
	Of terrifying wind and rain, she stole
	Outside, left my bed for the storm's frenzy;
	I followed her in anger and suspicion,
	A sword beneath my cloak. But no one came to her,
	Not a wolf ventured out of his den that night,
	As she was dancing in the gale's wild fury.
GWYDION:	Hard to draw a creature from its kindred.
LLEW:	I cried to her in terror, but she did not hear,
	As the wind was howling ruin through the trees.
	I was lost in an unintelligible world
	Where stone and rain could thrive, and storm and night,
	And she, Blodeuwedd. I went running after her,
	And cried still louder, and gripped her by the arm:
	"You have caught me," she said sadly, like someone waking
	From a far-off dream, "You have caught me, yes, let us go home."
	And it was then I saw, amid that tempest,
	There was nothing in her life that I could share.
GWYDION:	Here is Blodeuwedd.
	(She approaches slowly.)
LLEW:	Ah, why is there a heart of ice
	Within breasts that kindle love like June's
	First sunrise.

BLODEUWEDD:	My lord, I received your message.
LLEW:	Yes, my lady, we must be on our way.
BLODEUWEDD:	And Gwydion as well?
GWYDION:	I, too, my lady.
BLODEUWEDD:	The day is short, and it will soon be night. My lord, stay here for now, I do not want to be Without you tonight.
LLEW:	You will not be alone, You have a host of maids and servants.
BLODEUWEDD:	I have never been without you before. I am afraid of your leaving me.
LLEW:	When did this start?
BLODEUWEDD:	My spirit is uneasy. Nothing good will come Of your leaving today. Wait till dawn is young. You will have sunshine on your way to Caer Dathal.
LLEW:	No, no. Everyone is ready; we must go With Math, the king himself, expecting us.
BLODEUWEDD:	*(turning to Gwydion)* My lord sorcerer, am I beautiful?
GWYDION:	What conjuring tricks are these?
BLODEUWEDD:	No conjuring, no tricks. You took my spirit captive among the leaves: Tell me, was your work done well?
GWYDION:	By my sword, Eyes have seen nothing lovelier than you, girl, You are the masterpiece of all my magic.
BLODEUWEDD:	Why, then, when I ask this of my husband, The only favour I have ever sought, Will he not grant it?
GWYDION:	The only favour, niece?
BLODEUWEDD:	The only one.
GWYDION:	You have been a fool, Blodeuwedd. You should have trained him well with your demands And worn his soul out with a thousand whims; That is how you get men to grant favours.
BLODEUWEDD:	Yes, The peasant girls know more than I of men. Lord Gwydion, you did me harm

	When you laid chains of flesh and bones upon me;
	No thanks to you for that, I ought to hate you.
	But instinct in me makes me fond of you;
	You also have spent summers under the leaves
	And know the tang of wild and cunning creatures.
GWYDION:	Hush. No mention of that; it would shame me.
BLODEUWEDD:	O my friend, what is shame? I do not know
	How it is to be ashamed . . . Stay here
	Until my lord comes back to me.
	You will be my safety during all that time.
	(A servant stands at the door.)
SERVANT:	My lord, the escort is awaiting you,
	Mounted and ready.
LLEW:	Yes, let us go.
	Come, my friend, it is time for us to start.
GWYDION:	Farewell, my lady. I am old,
	And you would grow weary of my grey company.
	The fragrances of May are all about you.
	Unfaded the blossoms woven in your face.
	Be young forever: farewell.
BLODEUWEDD:	My gracious lord,
	Will the three of us ever be together again?
	My heart is heavy. Farewell . . .
	(Gwydion leaves)
	My Llew,
	If you trusted me, you would not start today;
	I know in my bones no good will come from this.
LLEW:	I cannot rule my life by a woman's whims.
BLODEUWEDD:	I have more knowledge of the seasons than you,
	And the changes of wind and rain and fair weather —
	Then how could I not know a human season?
LLEW:	Do not be afraid. I am so destined
	No evil or harm will easily come to me.
	And be prudent. Do not stray far from home,
	Do not go to the lonely woodland in the evening,
	But stay within the walks of settled places
	With your maids beside you. Take heart,
	Blodeuwedd,

	I will only be three days. Farewell, farewell.
	(Exit. Blodeuwedd flings herself on a couch and weeps. Rhagnell, her maid, enters and find her this way.)
RHAGNELL:	Blodeuwedd, my lady, why are you so distressed? Blodeuwedd, answer me.
BLODEUWEDD:	My lord has left me.
RHAGNELL:	What if he has? It is only for three days. He will come back Very soon.
BLODEUWEDD:	Rhagnell, you do not know The fear that is in my heart.
RHAGNELL:	Calm yourself, my lady. What have you to fear? This is your castle, And the land is yours, and your word is its law, And there is no one here who does not love you. As for me, I would give my life for you If need be.
BLODEUWEDD:	No, no. No fear of men Disturbs me. But fears of emptiness, aloneness. My lord has gone away.
RHAGNELL:	What is this? I have often heard you wishing to escape, And your curse on the man who made you a wife: What has changed?
BLODEUWEDD:	O, you will never understand My anguish, never, not you, not anyone. You do not know what it is to be alone. For you the world is full, you have a home, Kinsmen and family, father, mother, brothers, And so you are not a stranger in the world. The spot where men have walked is familiar, And all of Gwynedd, where your forefathers lived, Is a hearth to you, a roof constructed By generations of your ancestors: You are at home in your own land As in a bed that was prepared for you By loving hands that long awaited you; As for me, not a single homestead is mine

	In all the paths of men; search Gwynedd there
	And the lengths of Britain, not a single grave
	Belongs to me, and the world is cold,
	Alien to me, without bond of kindred
	Or link of race. That is my sort of fear —
	Fearing my freedom, like a rudderless ship
	On humanity's ocean. Listen, what is that horn?
	(A hunting horn is heard far off)
RHAGNELL:	Someone hunting in the woodland over there.
BLODEUWEDD:	My lord has gone away. No, there has never
	Been affection between us. He knows nothing
	Of the tangled passions that are in my nature,
	And I do not know how to live tamely like him,
	Taking no chances, and relying on friends
	All his life for every good thing he has gained.
	Yet he among men is the only one
	Related to me. There is no one else
	As a link between me and the high-born men
	Who honour nothing but lineage. Without him
	My life is without family, without anchor,
	Nature's defiance and peril in my blood.
	Now God take my part to shield me from vengeance
	When this evil comes upon us.
RHAGNELL:	What evil, my lady?
	Your words are frightening me. Let me know
	What wild tempest is raging within your flesh?
	(The horn sounds nearer)
BLODEUWEDD:	Hush, listen.
RHAGNELL:	Yes, the hunt is coming this way.
BLODEUWEDD:	*(Drawing the maid to her and placing a hand on her heart)*
	Rhagnell, where is your heart? Ah, as tranquil
	As the heart of an oak in rain-drenched winter.
	(The horn sounds, very close)
	Listen, girl. A hunting horn. Hunting among the trees
	And the stag lashing the earth churning behind him
	Like oars striking the wave. The hounds are leaping
	Snuffing along the trail, and the horses' hooves

                Are like the wind along the miles. O nature there
                Is in spendthrift joy at a revel of life,
                And the hunter is one with the moorland's
                    vigour —
                I could love a hunter —
                (The horn goes past)
                Go, girl, go,
                And ask who is this knight that comes hunting.
RHAGNELL: *(After going out, returning to the door)*
                My lady, the hunt is over, and the lord
                Is coming this way across the moor.
                Would it not be right to offer him lodging,
                With night closing in on him?
BLODEUWEDD: What is he like?
RHAGNELL: Young, and as easy on his horse
                As a hawk upon the breeze.
BLODEUWEDD: Bring me
                Goblets of gold, and the wine I tasted
                The dawn I was created, and bring me fruits,
                Cherries and apples, red and sweet,
                And go to greet the knight;
                Have his clothing attended to. Bring him
                Water for washing, and lead him to the hall.
                And command a banquet tonight for this stranger
                Or else my lord may find fault with me
                For letting him go, as day fades, to his homeland.
RHAGNELL: There now, my lady, this is how you should be,
                Cheerful and gracious. I will go
                To receive him, and order tables piled high
                As a welcome for him. And you, be merry,
                Forget your sorrows. Banquet and dance
                And gracious words are your sisters,
                And all who see you are your kinsmen.
                (She leaves)
BLODEUWEDD: Be quiet, troubled heart, your time has come . . .
                Though I have bowed for a year beneath a court's
                    customs
                And the ways of men, these confine me no longer,
                My elements are freedom and excitement,

	And my law is lust, the lust that drives the seed
	To thrust through the soil that keeps it from the sun.
	There is a shoot in me that longs for a day
	To swell fruitful and full-branched above the grove
	With no one's knife to prune it. And I know
	That this knight is passion's herald to me.
	I know the music of a horn: it was not
	My husband's thin lips blew that lusty call,
	But full lips, red, devouring, drunken,
	My own lips' proper partners.
RHAGNELL:	*(At the door)*
	My lady, the feast is ready, and Gronw Pebr,
	The Lord of Penllyn, sends you his greetings.
BLODEUWEDD:	How barren are your words. A brazen trumpet,
	Not the tongue of a girl, should announce that name.
	Give me your arm: let us go to welcome him.

(They go. The light is lowered to signify the time passed at the banquet. Then light again, the scene as before, except that there are wine-cups and flowers on the table. Blodeuwedd and Gronw Pebr enter.)

BLODEUWEDD:	Have you had your fill?
GRONW:	Yes, of food and drink.
BLODEUWEDD:	What else is there?
GRONW:	Do not ask, my lady.
BLODEUWEDD:	You fear to speak.
GRONW:	The only fear I know
	Is of losing dignity and honour.
BLODEUWEDD:	Fear never captured a stag or a woman.
GRONW:	My lady, is there a way from here tonight?
BLODEUWEDD:	Yes, across the hills where the swift-running wolves
	Are howling of their famine to the moon.
GRONW:	Can one of your servants show me the path?
BLODEUWEDD:	No one but I would dare to do that.
GRONW:	You?
BLODEUWEDD:	The night and I are long-acquainted,
	And wolves will not chase the scent of flowers.

GRONW: Is it true that you were created from wildflowers?
BLODEUWEDD: *(Taking the flowers from the table)*
Do you see these blossoms? They are so serene,
You would say their beauty is eternal;
And yet they are dying. They were plucked
And set there for a time to grace a feast,
And so arranged, held up, but robbed of roots;
There is pain already in their stricken hearts
And weariness in their stems. They will start to droop,
And shed their weight of colour to the floor
And dry and wither and die before their time . . .
My lord, would you say that I am beautiful?
GRONW: The rose of the world.
BLODEUWEDD: And yet, I am withering,
I have no root or earth among mankind.
There is water to spare these flowers' pain
And prolong their end; but I was picked
By an arrogant hand and put here to die
Without one kind element to keep me young.
GRONW: What is your will?
BLODEUWEDD: Tell me your secret,
And I shall tell you after that my will.
GRONW: When I first looked at you, I loved you.
BLODEUWEDD: And because of that you wished to leave me?
GRONW: You are married, and I sat and ate
At your husband's table. Was there not
An obligation that I had to him?
BLODEUWEDD: And now?
GRONW: O, I am so lost in love of you
I no longer know of dignity or honour.
Your face, my dearest, is the castle of marvels
That has charmed me to forget all forms of law
And noble birth's fidelity. To me you are
The end of hope, the haven of my dreams
Where I will cast my wild youth's anchor.
BLODEUWEDD: No more begging to leave?
GRONW: Never, never again.

BLODEUWEDD: And your rank and your tradition, your family
Courtesy, and noble blood's fidelity?
GRONW: I will forget them.
BLODEUWEDD: No, forget nothing,
Or else they might come to mind again sometime
And chill the blood and consume the flames of desire.
But make your choice between us, sweet, between them,
The tame safe ways of man's civilization
And the full tempest of my kisses.
And think before you make your choice. With them
Yours is the certainty of kinsman, friend, and wife,
Spending an untroubled life on your estate,
And burial in your upright forebears' grave,
Your children carrying your bier. With me
Nothing is secure except this minute.
The man who loves me, that man must love peril
And all the loneliness of freedom. He will have
No friends in his lifetime, no children will escort him
To his unvisited grave. But my hair's heavy shower
Will flood his senses for a time, and my breasts
Hide him a while from the murmurs of the world,
And the moment will be his heaven . . . Make your choice.
GRONW: Who knows his future? What does it pay a man
To lose his joy tonight for a tomorrow
Hope alone can see? Tonight is being, is a gift;
We have been tossed together; shall I go away
And leave this as if my life once had a dream
And reject the hour of the gods? I have made my choice:
Your beauty as a ruler in my heart,
Your will on my life's throne hereafter.
BLODEUWEDD: My will is wholly given to love's passion . . .
(She pours wine into a cup)
Listen, my dear: the day I was taken captive

               And bound fast in my husband's court and bed,
Gwydion gave me a wine, marvellous in flavour,
Pryderi brought from Annwn long ago. I
Tasted it and kept it, and swore an oath
Not to drink it again until an hour came
Of feasting with a man that I had chosen
Freely, gladly. The bowl has long been locked away;
I have often thirsted for its special savour.
But today, this evening, I heard a horn
There in the woods, that rang like a king's challenge
Ending months of captivity, and I knew
The mouth that sent a summons through the grove
Would drink with me from passion's cup . . .
(She drinks and gives him her cup.)
Drink, Gronw, there is my seal upon the rim.

GRONW: I will drink, and swear to you a love that lasts . . .

BLODEUWEDD: No, my dearest, do not swear to me.
Leave making vows to those
Who safeguard feeble passions with the rites
And the fearful bonds of their barren creeds.
What would promises be but an admission
That this hour's bliss is not enough for us?
Be tranquil in our night of joy,
Not doubting what may come. All the power
Of nature gathers in me to satisfy you.
And if I do not tire, you will not tire.

GRONW: *(Drinking)*
Let this cup your lips have touched
Be a foretaste of your kisses. This night
I could wish to die in your arms, my girl,
Rather than wake in a tomorrow without you.

BLODEUWEDD: Rhagnell, Rhagnell . . .
(Rhagnell enters.)
Make my bed tonight
In the glass chamber, and lay upon it
The whitest, smoothest linen, just as it was
On the very first night I ever slept.
(Rhagnell leaves.)
My sweet, what did you see in me to attract you?

GRONW: Who can ever say? Your face, your form, your movements,
And your body blazing like a flame through your gown.
BLODEUWEDD: And was there nothing else? Could you not see
The wonder of my birth? Before you came,
This body was a prison that encompassed me,
Like a dead web around a living butterfly;
And then you came like spring where I was lying
And gave wings to my flesh, put a dance in my blood.
From now on I will not be lonely among families;
Your smiles are my lineage and the claim I make
On humanity. There is a single will
In leaves and men; no fragile ceremony,
Custom or decree can enslave the heart that feels
The striking of passion's shafts. Come, my darling:
Life is ours, and to love is to be free.

CURTAIN

ACT II

Three days later. The castle in Ardudwy. Rhagnell, Blodeuwedd's maid, is there, and Gronw's Captain.

CAPTAIN: Rhagnell, where is my lord?
RHAGNELL: I do not know.
CAPTAIN: *(Scornfully)* Just as you do not know of the doings between him and your lady?
RHAGNELL: Are there doings?
CAPTAIN: How is it, then, that you are the only one to wait on them? Why does he spend three days away from his homeland? Are there doings indeed?
RHAGNELL: He goes back this morning.
CAPTAIN: Yes, and the horses there are waiting for him. Go, tell him to bid goodbye to the half-breed sorceress who has bewitched him, and start for home.
RHAGNELL: He is in a bad way if he has no retainers more faithful than you.
CAPTAIN: What has he to do with fidelity? He will sell his father's home for the sake of his lust, and his only virtue is that he is too reckless to know fear . . . Hush, here they come . . . Will you say now there are no doings between them?
RHAGNELL: Be quiet, you lout.
(Gronow Pebr and Blodeuwedd enter.)
CAPTAIN: If you please, my lord, the horses are ready.
GRONW: Go to them. I will come before long.
(Exeunt Rhagnell and the Captain.)
BLODEUWEDD: Must you go?
GRONW: Or stay here to be killed.
BLODEUWEDD: No, my dearest. If there is to be killing,
You are not the one who shall be killed.

GRONW: His men are here,
And he is returning today with his escort.
BLODEUWEDD: Yes, go. Delay no longer. His name
Is like a death knell in my broken heart.
You know how, in the groves in June,
When the singing spills from blackbirds' beaks like golden grain,
And the sound of the leaves is louder than the sound of the brook,
Thwack, when no one expects it, comes a standstill,
The whistling stops on every branch and hedge
And the sap of trees goes numb within their trunks,
And that minute, the leaves begin to grow old,
Summer's heaviness and languor come over the grove,
And that is the death of spring. So it is with me,
In the middle of the first measure of my love's dance,
His name and the reminder that he exists
Make me stumble.
GRONW: Blodeuwedd, was it for this
I was charmed three days ago to search for you,
To see in you my joy and my fulfillment,
And then, without hope, to say farewell?
BLODEUWEDD: I have tasted joy as if a bite
Were hurting my breast, the pangs of love's birth,
And this, my body, that had been before
A dead cairn to me, see, it is now
A garden of all the scents of my life's spring,
A new world you struck with your magic rod
And planted with blessings. You, my dear,
Not Math or Gwydion, are my creator.
GRONW: Do you know all that is in your world?
BLODEUWEDD: Our bodies cannot be exhausted. O, my Gronw,
What a feat it would be to pierce all their riches,
The secret of the five awakened senses,
The seasons of our stillness, the peace of sleep

On a sweetheart's arm, the breathing as one.
Desire has the art to bind bodies together
And create a new, higher life between them
Greater than the two apart, where each one
Loses the constraint of being, and plays freely
In the ecstasy of passion's deeds. And for me
You are the door of this paradise. For without you
Nothing is left for me but weeping all night
And watching someone sleeping beside me,
A cold and foreign tyrant.

GRONW: You do not want
Today to mark the end of our passion?

BLODEUWEDD: I want to live. Lust and life are one;
I have seen the dawning of desire with you,
I want to see its noon.

GRONW: And Llew Llaw Gyffes?

BLODEUWEDD: Why did you name him? Was it not enough
To know he is like a predator between us
And the path of desire?

GRONW: We must look at our fear
And name it, so that we may not fear it.

BLODEUWEDD: Is there some way
To delude Llew?

GRONW: Yes. Escape with me
This morning.

BLODEUWEDD: Where?

GRONW: To my castle,
For here are the horses waiting at the gate
And freedom in the stirrup. Let Llew come
To his lair and find it empty. From my fortress walls
We will defy him safely, let him roar
Threats as he pleases.

BLODEUWEDD: You do not know
The power he has. Math will come with him
And behind him all the might of Gwynedd,
And Gwydion the sorcerer. No fort in the world
Can stand against them. I have no wish

| | To be caught like a deer in the claws of Llew
| | And have my flesh torn.
| GRONW: | Blodeuwedd, what is a court
| | Or a kingdom to us? Let us flee to Dyfed,
| | We will be welcomed there by Math's enemies,
| | And find support and safety.
| BLODEUWEDD: | I will never go.
| | I cannot go impoverished to foreign men.
| | It is easy for you to trust in strangers,
| | Since you are human like them. I have
| | No claim on anyone, no faith in his word.
| | I fear everything strange.
| GRONW: | Human beings
| | Are not as unkind as you believe.
| BLODEUWEDD: | Not to each other. But to me who am not
| | One of them, who will dare to give his trust?
| | And I in turn have no faith in them.
| | Unless he is linked to me in bonds of passion
| | Everyone is an enemy to me . . . My only brother,
| | Do not take me from here.
| GRONW: | What shall we do?
| BLODEUWEDD: | Kiss and forget and say farewell.
| GRONW: | That is your advice?
| BLODEUWEDD: | I know of no better.
| GRONW: | Will you find it easy to forget it all?
| BLODEUWEDD: | Forgetting takes no long apprenticeship. Its craft
| | Becomes easier every day.
| GRONW: | I can never forget.
| BLODEUWEDD: | Everyone is awkward when beginning his work,
| | Like a pupil at his task.
| GRONW: | Do you want
| | To forget?
| BLODEUWEDD: | Do you?
| GRONW: | When I want to die.
| BLODEUWEDD: | Kiss me, my dearest . . . It will not be long
| | Before he claims the tribute of my lips,
| | And his indifferent hand on my white shoulder
| | Has dominion over all my flesh.

	O why have I not poison in my teeth,
	Then like a serpent I would wind about his neck,
	Embracing him more warmly than I ever did . . .
	Like this . . . like this . . . I would sting him to death.
GRONW:	That is the only way — we must kill him.
BLODEUWEDD:	How long it has taken you to see my purpose.
GRONW:	I do not want to kill him unless we must.
BLODEUWEDD:	We must, we must. What place is there for him
	In a world that knows the tempest of our passion?
	A withered tree in the whirlwind's path.
GRONW:	Is there a way
	To kill him?
BLODEUWEDD:	It will not be easy. He is so fated
	That no one else can know the way to kill him;
	He himself knows it.
GRONW:	And is fate also
	An enemy of passion?
BLODEUWEDD:	Passion is a rare flower
	That grows on the precipice of death. A few snatch it,
	And the rest are like an ox chewing its cud in a field.
GRONW:	How beautiful is scorn upon your lips.
	There is a rose in the world more rare than passion,
	For otherwise, I would not risk my life
	Nor plot to betray the innocent . . . Tell me now,
	How can we learn the way to kill him?
BLODEUWEDD:	Leave that to me. These fingers have the skill
	To play with his famished body so cunningly
	That his doubts will be charmed into compassion
	And his silent secret lured from his breast.
	His anger is the sulking of a child,
	He will return today, lonely and uneasy,
	And I, I will kiss him . . .
GRONW:	And win as a reward
	His life's great secret?
BLODEUWEDD:	A life for a kiss,
	Is the price too high?

GRONW:	At this moment, If I were the one to make the choice, I would fly to you like a moth to the flame.
BLODEUWEDD:	Yes, my spirit is a blazing flame, And he will find, the first who kindled the fire, It will consume him . . . How shall we plan things afterwards?
GRONW:	The planning belongs to me. If by human hands He can be destroyed, send a message to me, And when the day arrives, I will number All the hours I have lost of your sweetness, And in the blow that will destroy him I will gather the longing of morning, noon, and night, And avenge them on his corpse. *(Rhagnell enters)*
RHAGNELL:	Your men, my lord, Are waiting for you, and the sun above the hill Shows the hours of safety almost spent.
GRONW:	We must say farewell.
BLODEUWEDD:	Will you keep your word?
GRONW:	Do you doubt my fidelity?
BLODEUWEDD:	O Gronw, what is your fidelity to me? Will you keep your lust? Lust is strong To hold a will like an arrow to its mark When fidelity's bow is rusty. Look at me, Fill your mouth with the savour of this kiss, And your nostrils with the scent of my breasts . . . Now go.
GRONW:	I will hear from you tonight?
BLODEUWEDD:	Before nightfall.
GRONW:	It is night for me now: My sun is setting. Sweetheart, farewell . . . *(Exit. Silence. The sound of horses leaving.* *Blodeuwedd sits on a couch.)*
RHAGNELL:	I saw the stir of dust on the horizon. He will be here before long.
BLODEUWEDD:	What did you say?

RHAGNELL:	Where do you wish me to have dinner served?
BLODEUWEDD:	For whom?
RHAGNELL:	For you and the Earl, your husband.
BLODEUWEDD:	In a grave.
RHAGNELL:	Is that the power you were speaking of
	To Gronw before he left? Come, my lady,
	Prepare to welcome him. And I will go
	To greet him for you at the gate . . .
BLODEUWEDD:	Yes, go
	And reveal to him all my secrets.
RHAGNELL:	You think that I am going to betray you?
BLODEUWEDD:	You are human, fruit of the womb like him.
RHAGNELL:	*(Kneeling beside her.)*
	I am your handmaid as long as I live.
BLODEUWEDD:	No, no, you cannot mock me. I know
	My face can stun a young man's soul
	And bind him to my will. You are a woman . . .
	And I will never have the power to chain you.
RHAGNELL:	But I am held by a different chain.
BLODEUWEDD:	*(Looking at Rhagnell and taking a plait of her hair and beginning to bind it around her throat.)*
	Yes, you have a chain as well, my maid,
	You are beautiful too, my girl. Your hair is like
	A golden rope that falls upon your back
	And soft as silk. But why
	Not wear it like a torque around your neck,
	A golden torque, as a gift from your mistress
	Rewarding your fidelity? With this
	Tight, tight around you, Rhagnell dear,
	You can lie forever mute and prudent
	And keep my secret undisclosed.
RHAGNELL:	*(Without moving and quietly)*
	You are hurting me. Are you going to kill me?
BLODEUWEDD:	*(Gazing into her face)*
	I long to bind your slender little neck
	With this silk, so that not one treacherous word
	Can ever escape the modest lips
	That many nights have kissed their mistress' hand.
	You have waited on me often, pretty Rhagnell,

	And taken care of me before I slept. Now I,
	I can take care of you, and give you sleep
	Quieter than I have ever known.
RHAGNELL:	*(Still not moving)*
	Alive or dead I will never betray you.
BLODEUWEDD:	You shall not have the chance, my gentle dear,
	I will bind your tongue and your pretty lips
	Beyond all temptation.
RHAGNELL:	Here is the Earl.
	(Llew Llaw Gyffes enters. Both women rise to greet him.)
LLEW:	Have I arrived before I was expected?
RHAGNELL:	No, sir,
	For I saw the dust of your troop on the hill,
	And I ran to bring the news to my lady.
LLEW:	I hurried in advance of all my soldiers
	To see Blodeuwedd first.
BLODEUWEDD:	*(Going to him)*
	Here I am.
LLEW:	My flawless wife.
BLODEUWEDD:	You travelled safely?
LLEW:	The marvel of your beauty is the same today
	As on that morning when you first walked towards me
	Between the dawn and the dew. My lovely girl,
	I did not know how strong your spell was till I missed you.
BLODEUWEDD:	You never were away from me before.
LLEW:	I will not leave again until I die.
BLODEUWEDD:	May those words be true.
LLEW:	What have you been doing while I was away?
BLODEUWEDD:	Ask Rhagnell . . . Tell him, girl,
	Here is your chance.
RHAGNELL:	Sir, ever since the time
	That Blodeuwedd first came to Ardudwy
	I have been with her day and night to serve her.
	I never saw a tear upon her cheeks
	Or moisture in her eyes; a quiet one
	And self-contained in sadness. But the hour

| | You went away from here, I came upon her
Sobbing over there upon the couch,
Her body aching with her pain and fear,
And her answer to each comfort that I whispered
Was only, "My lord has gone away."
| --- | --- |
| LLEW: | O, my wife,
Why could I never know you before?
(Exit Rhagnell) |
| BLODEUWEDD: | Forget all former sorrow. This reunion
Seals a new marriage-bond between us. |
| LLEW: | I thought that you were cold and unimpassioned;
I did not know that tears of longing
Could cloud the brightness of your lovely eyes.
Why did you hide your tenderness from me? |
| BLODEUWEDD: | I was given you, my lord, like plunder
And like a slave-girl, without choice and mute.
You did not learn to want me before you had me,
Nor plot the way to win me. In your castle
You have arms and brazen coats-of-mail
That have cost you fighting and sweat and blood:
You gaze at them, remember each one's day of strife,
And look for your valour's trace and your arm's mark
In the many dents in them. But I, never
Did I cost you an hour's trouble to capture me,
And that is why you took no pains to see
A bruise or dent or void within my breast
Or traces of your ardour on my heart. |
| LLEW: | You are my wife. By means of you I hoped
To establish my family line in Ardudwy,
Revering you with a father's love for his son's mother.
What greater love than that could anyone have? |
| BLODEUWEDD: | I was your wife before I was a woman.
You want the fruit before the flowers bloom,
But I am the woman made of flowers, Blodeuwedd. |
| LLEW: | Woman made of flowers, teach me by what means |

                I can make my way past all the petals
                And be buried like a bee within your breast.
                I too, dear, am alone in the world; like you
                I have been a stranger to a mother's arms.
                She cast me from her womb before my time
                And harried me through the years. In all my life
                I never felt a kiss before your kiss,
                Or the hands of a girl around my neck;
                I had no brother's or sister's tenderness.
                I feel the longing for your love, dearest,
                Teach me how to win you willingly,
                For does not love draw love to itself
                And heart draw heart? O my wife, my world,
                Why do you keep away from me?
BLODEUWEDD: No, sweet,
                I have kept back nothing of myself.
LLEW: You gave your body, but you kept your will.
BLODEUWEDD: I gave you my trust. You alone
                Are all I have on earth. What would I do
                If you were killed, with no husband, no one?
LLEW: Did Rhagnell tell the truth about you weeping?
                (She is silent)
                Blodeuwedd, look at me . . . Answer me . . .
                Why will you not answer? . . . Are you well?
BLODEUWEDD: The day you went away from me
                My heart was close to breaking from despair:
                I feared I would not see you again alive.
LLEW: Was your love for me as great as that?
BLODEUWEDD: You are the only family I have.
LLEW: Half my soul is yours. Now I know your love,
                And life at last will be a balm to me
                And your company serenity. We two,
                We shall raise ourselves a family in Ardudwy
                That will be like a grove around us. There the young
                Saplings will grow with the sturdy ancient trees,
                And we shall be like a snug and sheltered orchard
                And love the surrounding walls between us

	And the cold gusts of loneliness. You, my wife,
	You will no longer be an exile; I am
	Your father's house and your tribe, and unless I am
	killed . . .
BLODEUWEDD:	If you are killed?
LLEW:	My fairest love, do not be sad,
	Do not be troubled. To kill me is not easy,
	Since how I shall be killed is already fated
	And that will not come readily at human hands.
BLODEUWEDD:	You are unconcerned and thoughtless
	And soon enough you will forget. But I,
	My concern will never allow me to forget;
	Let me know your fate, that my breast
	May no longer ache with anxiety.
LLEW:	I will gladly tell you. A full year must be spent
	In fashioning the spear that is to strike me,
	And the work may only be done at the time
	Of the Sacrifice of the Mass on Sundays.
BLODEUWEDD:	Is that certain?
LLEW:	Absolutely certain.
	Neither can I be killed within a house,
	Nor on my horse, nor with my feet on land,
	But I must be standing on a water-trough
	That is on a river bank. If I were there,
	And were struck in the back with a poisoned spear,
	Whoever struck me in this way could kill me.
BLODEUWEDD:	Thank God, it will be easy
	To avoid that.
LLEW:	There have been many times, Blodeuwedd,
	When I have wished for my death. But now
	Life has a tang like an apple's tang on the teeth,
	And your love is the chair in Caer Siddi
	Where no one is plagued by illness or old age,
	And I am monarch there,
	No one and nothing will depose me now,
	Not fear, not longing, not even death itself,
	For the sovereignty of love is changeless.
BLODEUWEDD:	Is there anything that is changeless among men?

LLEW: Passion dies, because it is fragile
And as fleeting as youth. But love grows
Like an oak through the tempests of a lifetime,
And under it a home, a family flourish,
And a land's nobility and government.
Our love, my beautiful lady, will be
A certainty and roof-beam to Ardudwy,
A people's learning, a tribe's nursery.
And we shall be blessed with princes
Because of the firm concord of this hour.
(Rhagnell enters)
RHAGNELL: Sir, the water and the towels are ready,
If you wish to change and wash away the dust,
Since it is very close to dinner-time.
LLEW: I am coming, girl. And order a feast today
Like a wedding-feast in my house. Three days ago
I left this place with a heavy heart;
I have returned today to greater joy
Than I have ever known. This special day
Is like a flag of safety for my castle,
For I have learned the nature of a wife's fidelity.
(Exit Llew)
BLODEUWEDD: Rhagnell, I tried to kill you.
RHAGNELL: Yes, my lady.
BLODEUWEDD: Why did you not betray me then?
RHAGNELL: You are a woman, my lady, I too am a woman,
And I will not betray another woman's secret.
BLODEUWEDD: I cannot understand humans. Wherever they are,
I hear nothing but talk about traditions,
Fidelity and loyalty, family, breeding,
Tribe, country, or creed . . . Do you care for me?
RHAGNELL: You are simple, my lady, like a child,
And like a child destructive. Who could not,
Once they know you, feel compassion for you?
I have been given to you as a handmaid,
And while I live I will be faithful to you.
BLODEUWEDD: Forgive me. I know that you are wise
And have all the knowledge of the daughters of men.

	And I, my only wisdom is to crave
	And seek with all my power what I want.
	Will you be my messenger to Penllyn's Earl?
RHAGNELL:	Yes, my lady.
BLODEUWEDD:	Tell him this:
	He must fashion a spear of steel and poison,
	And work upon it only at the time
	Of the Sacrifice of the Mass on Sundays;
	He must spend a full year in fashioning it,
	And when the year is ended he must come
	And keep a tryst with me near Bryn Cyfergyr.
	Go, hurry, so that no one can see you.
	And give this ring to him as a token.
RHAGNELL:	*(Taking the ring)*
	Is that everything?
BLODEUWEDD:	Everything, girl.
RHAGNELL:	If he asks about you?
BLODEUWEDD:	Tell him
	How cheerful my lord is, and that today
	There is feasting and dancing and singing at court
	As on a holiday. Go now, do not delay.

CURTAIN

ACT III

One year later. A hill in the background. A trough or long water-basin in the centre on a river-bank. Gronw and his Captain enter to Blodeuwedd and Rhagnell.

GRONW: I have come, Blodeuwedd.
BLODEUWEDD: Promptly, my valiant warrior,
Before the sun has risen above Bryn Cyfergyr.
Do not touch me, Gronw.
GRONW: My beautiful flower,
I bear a year of thirsting for your lips,
A long abstinence from your arms. And you say,
Do not touch me.
BLODEUWEDD: I bear Llew's collar;
I have come here now from his arms.
GRONW: Into my arms?
BLODEUWEDD: Across his corpse.
While he is alive do not put your hand upon me
Lest your blow should fail. Is that the spear?
GRONW: I have worked on it Sunday by Sunday through the year
At the hour of the Sacrifice. This spear is costly,
There is a soul's damnation in its sting.
BLODEUWEDD: You fear that? There is a road back to Penllyn:
A man's fate is not like the single course of a river
Or a woman made of flowers. You have a choice.
GRONW: Do not mock me, woman. Your perilous beauty
Is the fate I have chosen Sunday by Sunday
Until this minute. A lengthy year has passed
Since I saw you; the roses withered, the rose-hips
Fell with the leaves; sun and moon have gone

	Through the rounds of the months: my days stood still,
	Exiled from the turning of the seasons
	And nailed to your lips. The fierceness of your kiss
	Is the death I have sharpened on my spear.
BLODEUWEDD:	My Gronw, the year has been easier for you than me;
	You could tend your passion, number memories
	In the fold of solitude, and yield to longing
	Without stifling a sigh or throttling a tear.
	Not a day or a night was safe for me
	But his body's weight and my hatred's burden
	Were bruising my breasts and erasing your imprint.
	I will not say more; tonight I can talk and talk,
	Tonight, tomorrow, the next day, and O, I shall be free,
	But this is the hour to strike.
GRONW:	What is your plan?
BLODEUWEDD:	This man is your captain?
GRONW:	Commander of Penllyn's guard;
	The men are there in the woods, a hundred knights,
	And this lord will lead them.
BLODEUWEDD:	My valiant captain,
	Llew Llaw Gyffes will be killed at this trough.
	Go to your horses. Be ready. The minute
	He is killed, your lord's hunting horn will ring out;
	Gallop to the fortress; Rhagnell will open the gate;
	Only a soldier or two will be there to be bested;
	Take possession and hold it until we come.
	Tomorrow we shall unite Ardudwy and Penllyn.
	Rhagnell, go and tell my lord
	That I am here on the bank of the river Cynfael
	In the shadow of Bryn Cyfergyr, by the goat-trough;
	And here, after the words between us last night,
	I wish to speak with him now.
	(Exeunt Rhagnell and the Captain)
GRONW:	Will he come?

BLODEUWEDD: Why will my fond husband not come
 To his cherished wife?
GRONW: What words between you last night?
BLODEUWEDD: A hint that will bring him hurrying to me now.
GRONW: How do I kill him?
BLODEUWEDD: It will not be hard.
 I shall hide you here beneath this hollow bank;
 He cannot be killed while his feet are on land,
 But he must be standing on a water-trough
 That is on a river bank. When you see him here
 Stomping in his pride upon the trough,
 Stand up and stab his back with the poisoned spear,
 Sound your hunting horn, and leap to your reward.
GRONW: I wonder if you can get him onto the trough?
BLODEUWEDD: Do not fail in your blow; I will not fail
 To make him stand upon the trough.
GRONW: I have had my blow aimed for a year
 And I cannot fail. His death is not
 The target. Beyond his corpse is your kiss,
 That is my assurance that my spear shall not fail.
 It wil need a long lifetime, Blodeuwedd, to slake
 The thirst I have developed beneath twelve moons.
 How long this year has been; how scant they seem,
 All the years of living that are now before us.
BLODEUWEDD: In a year it will be sweet to recall this morning.
GRONW: Will it be easy to tame Ardudwy and hold it peacefully?
BLODEUWEDD: Why not? Has there ever been a single country
 That did not think successful force deserved success?
GRONW: I have heard that everyone is pleased with him.
BLODEUWEDD: Kill him, and you will be no less welcome.
GRONW: Will none of them try to avenge his wrong?
BLODEUWEDD: Be savage and fearsome tomorrow: the rest of your life
 They will run like little dogs to kiss your hand.
GRONW: You have learned the craft of ruling, my lady.
BLODEUWEDD: The flea has the instinct to rule; she and I

	Need only follow nature.
	Hush, hide yourself, my hunter, Llew is on the way.
	Bind your will to my will
	To lift him onto the trough. The last encounter comes:
	Then we can laugh and live as we please.
	(Blodeuwedd sits on the edge of the trough after Gronw hides. Llew comes to her.)
LLEW:	You rose early, my lady.
BLODEUWEDD:	The tremor of dawn
	Lured me like a rabbit to bathe in the grass.
LLEW:	And you came as barefoot as a rabbit too?
BLODEUWEDD:	It takes a married man to notice such a thing;
	Will you make me shoes as you did for your mother?
LLEW:	My mother did not walk in the dew, she was cautious;
	She sent servants with her foot-size.
BLODEUWEDD:	Was that the time you killed a wren with your spear?
LLEW:	Not a spear, a needle — no one could pierce a tiny wren with a spear;
	But a cobbler's needle I used to stitch her a shoe.
BLODEUWEDD:	A needle, to be sure. That was stupid of me.
	But tell me how it was you killed the wren.
LLEW:	Yes, gladly. But tell me first
	Why you have summoned me from bed so early.
BLODEUWEDD:	First the story of the wren.
LLEW:	No, your story first:
	Why did you summon me here outside the fort?
BLODEUWEDD:	After that the story of the killing of the little wren?
LLEW:	Yes, I promise, but what is this great secret?
BLODEUWEDD:	How persistent you are. Did I not tell you last night?
LLEW:	You said you would keep some joyful news till today
	To celebrate the day I came back from Caer Dathal.
BLODEUWEDD:	How slow your imagination is this morning . . .
	Does this past year make you contented, my lord?

LLEW: How could I not be contented? I have found a nest
In your trust; you have been tame and gentle,
Not like a wild bird trapped in a cage.
BLODEUWEDD: You still have fear of all wild things, my Llew?
LLEW: My mother was wild. I learned hatred from my mother.
She has harried me as a child and as a man,
And I do not know who my father was. All wild things are savage,
Craven and slavish, killing a man from behind.
You have been like a garden to me; never before
Have I spent a year unafraid of treachery's knife.
BLODEUWEDD: You have now overcome all your mother's dooms?
LLEW: Every one she named. There is one she did not name.
BLODEUWEDD: What is that, my dear? You gained a name;
You gained arms in spite of her; you gained a wife.
LLEW: When my mother laid a curse upon me
That I could never get a wife among the daughters of men,
Though her spell was thwarted and a woman created from flowers,
And given to me as the fairest maid in the world,
Though the spot where you stand is day's own sun
And at night it is sweet to hold you in my arms,
Though I give thanks for you, my lovely Blodeuwedd,
I know I have still not escaped my mother's rage.
BLODEUWEDD: Yes, I understand. But answer this:
When will you ever be free of her malice?
LLEW: When you tell me the best news I have ever heard.
BLODEUWEDD: And that news, sweet?
LLEW: The good news
That you are giving me a son, an heir.
BLODEUWEDD: And that will loose you from your mother's bonds?
LLEW: My mother tried to kill me. She failed to do it.
My birth was her disgrace, and by means of me
She spat her bile and spite upon the world.
She cut me off from men, from the body's

                 Ecstasy, and from a young man's joy,
Denying me arms, denying me a wife.
I have fought for life against her,
For a taste of the sweet things of man's communion;
Gwydion has been a father to me, you a wife;
From Math, the king, I have obtained lordship;
I know the ordinary troubles, and thanks to you,
This year, I know tenderness. The nightmare that has been
Is fading from my consciousness. But, Blodeuwedd,
If once I saw between your arms and breast
A boy, my heir, then the final chain
Would fall, I would be whole, the father
Of a family, a giver of life to generations.

BLODEUWEDD: Without that, you will not be content with me?
LLEW: Without that, I will be content; with that,
My love and thanks will turn to song around you.
BLODEUWEDD: Not a song for me, it would not be that,
But your triumphal ode against your mother.
Ah god, my Llew, if once you would look at me
And say: "You, you are my fulfillment."
If you would say that —
LLEW: I will say it when your son is on your arm.
BLODEUWEDD: A word like fate! Listen to my secret:
Here and now I have an heir for you.
LLEW: Do you know for certain?
BLODEUWEDD: As every woman knows.
LLEW: O my queen! Fate ordain it be a boy.
BLODEUWEDD: He is a boy, I swear it.
LLEW: I did not dare
Believe the meaning of your hint last night.
My cup is full; let death come when he will,
No bitter welcome shall he have from me.
BLODEUWEDD: Death will not come to you easily; the final fate
Is a strong fort to keep you from your mother's spear.
LLEW: My mother's rage is powerless when the boy arrives.
Imagine, my dear, the sort of heir he will be.

BLODEUWEDD: His kisses ardent; I imagine him now
Pressing his lips on my lips,
And he will be a hunter, his horn arousing the deer,
And dancing on Ardudwy's floor in his zest.
LLEW: I will teach him his father's boyhood games.
BLODEUWEDD: Will you teach him to hurl a spear and a needle?
LLEW: And to row a boat and make shoes for his mother
To keep her from walking barefoot in the dew.
BLODEUWEDD: Will you tell him the story of piercing the wren?
LLEW: I think I see him now as a three-year-old
Listening on his mother's lap to Gwydion's tales;
That wizard will enjoy amazing the little one
With the story of the boat at Arianrhod's castle.
BLODEUWEDD: Tell the story as if to your heir,
Suppose for now that this trough is the boat;
Where did Gwydion stand?
LLEW: Here, in the middle,
Bending towards my mother's foot.
BLODEUWEDD: And the nameless youth
Stitching the leather, where did you sit?
LLEW: There in the stern.
BLODEUWEDD: Did your mother look at you?
LLEW: Yes, long and hard, with her lip curled.
BLODEUWEDD: But without
Recognising you?
LLEW: Gwydion had cast a spell on us;
She was beautiful, her foot on the edge of the boat,
And she stood proudly, without stooping, like a princess.
BLODEUWEDD: Like this, was it, with her foot to the sea?
And then?
LLEW: It was spring; ten yards from the shore
Was a row of stones; through a low cleft there
I saw the wren darting in and out
On its sudden flights, then growing weary
And wanting a rest, and lighting on the bow of the boat.
BLODEUWEDD: Here? O show us how it stood.

LLEW: *(Leaping onto the front of the trough and standing looking out)*
Now look . . .
(Blodeuwedd moves to left centre stage and faces him. Gronw Pebr stands up on the right behind him, and aims the spear.)
Mother and Gwydion were here,
And I in the stern. There was a moment of
    tenseness,
A shiver of stillness upon the water,
And there was the wren. It stood and raised its wing
Like this . . . its head down . . . And at that second,
The needle between my fingers —

BLODEUWEDD: A needle, not a spear —
LLEW: I aimed at him —
GRONW: Like this.
(He thrusts the spear into Llew's back. Llew falls with a cry to the ground face down. They look at him.)

GRONW: Is he dead?
BLODEUWEDD: He quivered and tossed his head
Twice on the grass and grew still. He is still now.
GRONW: The poison cannot fail. All of Gwydion's
Sorcery could not turn aside this fate.
(He sounds his hunting horn. A sound of horses is heard in the distance.)
BLODEUWEDD: Come, my heir . . .
(They embrace. Blodeuwedd laughs wildly.)
He is a boy, I swear it.
GRONW: I never saw a better end to a story . . .
Yes, he is dead.
BLODEUWEDD: How easily a man dies.
GRONW: Look, there is sunlight on the hill.
BLODEUWEDD: Let us wait a while;
I did not believe he could die so easily.
GRONW: Let us go to the fort to take possession.
BLODEUWEDD: He gave a scream and was gone;
Is this how it will be for me when my turn comes?
GRONW: Come, Blodeuwedd. This is no time to linger.

BLODEUWEDD: I never saw dying before. What shall we do with him?
GRONW: I will send soldiers to bury him this afternoon.
BLODEUWEDD: Hush! I heard a noise in the woods like the ring of a shield.
GRONW: They have probably left one on guard.
BLODEUWEDD: Has his spirit fled in anger to the woods?
GRONW: His spirit cannot ring like a shield.
BLODEUWEDD: He dropped like a flower. Is this the way
You will die?
GRONW: Come, my girl,
You are like an owl, not your lively self.
We must hold the fort, take swift control of the land,
And then we shall be safe. Let us go quickly.
(Exeunt. A moment of stillness. Then two soldiers, and Gwydion afterwards, slip in cautiously. They find Llew.)
SOLDIER: This is worse than your fears, my lord Gwydion:
Here is your nephew, a corpse by the trough . . .
GWYDION: Is this where you fell, my child,
Like a great wounded eagle? Come to my lap . . .
His heart has stopped beating. O evil woman . . .
Let us lift him, men; we will carry him to the woods
And hide him under the oak trees. There my cunning
Can struggle for him with that sorcerer, death.
Steady now . . . gently . . . very quietly . . .

CURTAIN

ACT IV

One year later, in the castle hall. The Captain and Rhagnell.

CAPTAIN:	You are still the only one here, Rhagnell?
RHAGNELL:	Only me. My lady is not yet up.
CAPTAIN:	In Llew's days she would be the first one up. Has Gronw returned from hunting?
RHAGNELL:	No.
CAPTAIN:	Some of the men are back. I saw them in the courtyard.
RHAGNELL:	Not much zest in their hunting, I would say.
CAPTAIN:	There is zest in the whispers among them now.
RHAGNELL:	If they have tales, they should save them for the feast.
CAPTAIN:	What feast?
RHAGNELL:	What feast? Where have you come from?
CAPTAIN:	From roaming Arfon and scouting Dyffryn Nantlle; I heard not so much as a word about a feast there.
RHAGNELL:	A year ago today Gronw came to Ardudwy, And I opened the gates of the castle for you.
CAPTAIN:	Will you be gatekeeper today?
RHAGNELL;	Stop your worthless chatter.
CAPTAIN:	You will marvel at the guests who will come to your feast.
RHAGNELL;	Why must you torment me? I have done you no harm.
CAPTAIN:	You have opened too many doors in your time.
RHAGNELL;	And you and your lord came through every one of them.
CAPTAIN:	I will not come this afternoon.
RHAGNELL;	An evil omen:

	Penllyn's soldiers will flee from a battle sooner than a feast.
CAPTAIN:	Who will be welcomed here from Caer Dathal? Was Gwydion invited?
RHAGNELL;	I would scarcely think so.
CAPTAIN:	I heard in Nantlle he was on his way.
RHAGNELL;	Perhaps you heard that Llew Llaw Gyffes was on the way?
CAPTAIN:	Yes, I heard that as well.
RHAGNELL:	You stupid liar.
CAPTAIN:	Liar, fair enough. But why call me stupid?
RHAGNELL:	You yourself are the one who buried Llew.
CAPTAIN:	I have often heard that said.
RHAGNELL:	You said it, no one else.
CAPTAIN:	Did you hear me?
RHAGNELL;	When the earl and my lady came from the slaughter He commanded you and two of your soldiers To bury the body near the goat-trough. We were sitting at the marriage-feast an hour or more Before you arrived and said that your task was done.
CAPTAIN:	Did Gronw or anyone else ask what task that was?
RHAGNELL;	Was it not to bury Llew?
CAPTAIN:	Have you seen the grave?
RHAGNELL:	No.
CAPTAIN:	Has your lady seen it?
RHAGNELL:	I do not know.
CAPTAIN:	Strange that no one has asked about the grave.
RHAGNELL:	Taming Ardudwy and winning its obedience Was more urgent than putting stones on a grave.
CAPTAIN:	There is comfort in a grave, a sign that a dead man is there. Stones on an enemy's grave give sleep to the living.
RHAGNELL;	No need to fear, Gronw is a splendid sleeper.
CAPTAIN:	Does he sleep as soundly as Llew by the goat-trough?
RHAGNELL:	What do you mean?
CAPTAIN:	Did you not say It was there that Llew Llaw Gyffes died?

RHAGNELL: He bore a fate that such was the way he would die.
CAPTAINL No, but a fate that he could only be killed that way.
RHAGNELL: Two and two make four. He was killed, he died.
CAPTAIN: And since you are certain of that, be glad.
RHAGNELL: I certain? You are the one who buried him.
CAPTAIN: You said that already. I do not know why.
RHAGNELA; You do not know? Did you not bury him?
CAPTAIN: It has been a year since Llew Llaw Gyffes was lost
And not one person has ever asked that before.
RHAGNELL: What need was there to ask when everyone knew it?
CAPTAIN: I did not know it.
RHAGNELL: How is that? Not know it?
CAPTAIN: If he was buried, he was not buried by me.
RHAGNELL: Your soldiers, then, at your command?
CAPTAIN: Go, ask them. There they are in the courtyard.
RHAGNELL: Llew Llaw Gyffes was killed at the goat-trough.
CAPTAIN: That was my understanding; I went there;
There was neither corpse nor goat near the spot;
I searched the woods and the river, and searched in vain.
RHAGNELL: Why did you not tell that to Gronw Pebr?
CAPTAIN: That man has never told the truth to anyone;
It does not pay to tell him the truth before one must.
RHAGNELL: Probably one of his men took the body away?
CAPTAIN: Strange that Gwydion did not come from Caer Dathal
Or a bard from Arfon to sing above his grave.
I heard no lament in Nantlle, nor his mother crowing.
RHAGNELL: You mean that Llew Llaw Gyffes is alive?
CAPTAIN: That is what I thought. I went to Arfon;
Gwydion and Math's physicians all this year
Have been fighting with the poison for Llew's life.
Now he is alive and well. He will be here today:
He has a word or two for Gronw Pebr.
RHAGNELL: I would not be surprised. Does he have company?
CAPTAIN: His uncle Gwydion and three hundred armed men.

(Blodeuwedd comes towards them.)

RHAGNELL: There is news, my lady.
BLODEUWEDD: Cheerful or foolish?
RHAGNELL: Is it cheerful or foolish that Llew is alive?
BLODEUWEDD: Alive? Who has said so?
CAPTAIN: I saw him yesterday.
BLODEUWEDD: Ha, the day has come . . . I was expecting this.
CAPTAIN: Expecting it, my lady? For how long?
BLODEUWEDD: From that moment, a year ago to the day,
I saw your hesitant face peer in at the gate
The day Ardudwy and Penllyn were united;
There was mockery in your eyes and on your lips.
CAPTAIN: I have never done you wrong, my lady.
BLODEUWEDD: You kept silence out of hatred for me, a lying silence,
Plotting the fall and ruin of my frail paradise.
You did not bury Llew.
CAPTAIN: No, not I.
BLODEUWEDD: Gwydion snatched him away.
CAPTAIN: How do you know?
BLODEUWEDD: I know my sorcerer's hand. He alone
Could pluck from Annwn swine or the soul of a man
And spellbind death. Does he come here today?
CAPTAIN: Gwydion and Llew with three hundred men.
BLODEUWEDD: Come what may, I have had my hour.
CAPTAIN: What is your advice, my lady? The time is short.
BLODEUWEDD: Should I advise someone preparing betrayal?
CAPTAIN: I will swear —
BLODEUWEDD: That you have already arranged your flight.
CAPTAIN: Scarcely forty men cannot hold the castle.
BLODEUWEDD: Saddles on the horses, the din of shields,
All the hustle and bustle of leaving, and the earl in the woods
Unwarned, and the avenger in his land.
CAPTAIN: I sent searchers after him, I posted lookouts —
BLODEUWEDD: You arranged everything to escape before he came.
CAPTAIN: He must escape, and you. The soldiers will refuse

	To wait for the enemy here in Ardudwy;
	There in Penllyn right and might are ours.
BLODEUWEDD:	Is it for soldiers to make their lord's decision?
CAPTAIN:	Is that worse for him than being a woman's slave?
BLODEUWEDD:	How easy it was to whip your treason to your mouth
	And hook it to your tongue, deceitful Captain.
CAPTAIN:	Trading taunts with you is pointless, with the enemy at hand —

(Gronw enters.)

RHAGNELL:	Gronw Pebr is here, my lady, now.
BLODEUWEDD:	Have you heard, Gronw?
GRONW:	Yes, everything.
BLODEUWEDD:	Your captain has arranged our flight to Penllyn.
GRONW:	And our own soldiers?
CAPTAIN:	Not forty men are here,
	And some of those are tenants in Ardudwy
	Whose loyalty cannot be trusted.
GRONW:	You were wise to muster the men and the horses,
	The fort cannot be held.
CAPTAIN:	That is a soldier's speech,
	Not a wench's babble when the battle is near.
GRONW:	Are the men ready?
CAPTAIN:	Men and horses,
	And fresh horses for you and for your lady.
GRONW:	How soon will the enemy be here?
CAPTAIN:	I have posted lookouts,
	We will know when the enemy reaches the glen.
GRONW:	You have always been shrewd and tenacious.
	I give you possession of the land of Penllyn
	And the heritage to you and to your children,
	And I give you custody of this lady
	And Rhagnell, her maid; grant them a refuge
	From Gwydion's terror, from Llew's claw;
	And send ambassadors to Caer Dathal
	To Math, the king, and offer recompense
	To keep him from bringing carnage to your land;
	Rule your country more wisely than I have done.

| | I will remain here to satisfy
Llew Llaw Gyffes for his shame and dishonour;
And so you can safely make your escape. |
| --- | --- |
| CAPTAIN: | My lord, you need not do that. There in Penllyn
You have men and a fortress and the right to rule. |
| GRONW: | Do as I have said. I will stand
Here to welcome Llew to his lair. |
| BLODEUWEDD: | My Gronw, what is this? |
| GRONW: | Go, Rhagnell, hurry
To gather your lady's things for the journey.
(Exit Rhagnell.) |
| BLODEUWEDD: | But you will come also, Gronw? |
| GRONW: | No, I will not.
I have long been mindless; I am mindless no more.
I will not bring vengeance on my innocent people
Or destroy my father's home. |
| BLODEUWEDD: | Let us flee to Dyfed,
We will be welcomed there by Math's enemies,
And find support and safety. |
| GRONW: | If I did that,
Math would spit his rage on the splendour of Penllyn,
While I fled, afraid, in a woman's arms. |
| CAPTAIN: | It came to you late, my lord, the memory of Penllyn,
But come now and you will find your country with you. |
| GRONW: | Your rebuke, sir, is fair, your offer fair,
And fair is my refusal. I owe a debt
To Llew of Ardudwy, and I will pay it today
Here, myself, asking no one for surety. |
| CAPTAIN: | I ask you now as a soldier, my lord:
The time is short to save the men's lives,
We must choose a fight here or escape through the woods
Before the enemy closes the cwm; they move on horseback. |
| GRONW: | It does not pay to waver — |

BLODEUWEDD: Gronw, my Gronw —
GRONW: Do not touch me, woman, our time has come
 To say farewell; you have a journey ahead of you.
BLODEUWEDD: I will make no journey from here without you
 Or leave you alone in Gwydion's hands.
GRONW: Your husband is alive. He will be here. You cannot stay.
BLODEUWEDD: I cannot go alone to foreign men,
 They will kill me without you.
GRONW: My brave captain,
 I have given you my lordship. Give me your oath
 That this lady will take her place unscorned
 In Penllyn under your protection.
 (The sound of a trumpet outside. A soldier rushes in.)
SOLDIER: Sir, the enemy vanguard is entering the glen.
CAPTAIN: Mount, everyone! Come now, my lord.
GRONW: Hurry, Blodeuwedd. Where is Rhagnell, your maid?
SOLDIER: Rhagnell went out of the fort just now.
GRONW: Out? Where?
SOLDIER: I do not know; towards the river.
CAPTAIN: This is no time for anyone to look for a grave.
GRONW: You cannot stay for her.
BLODEUWEDD: I must stay,
 Do not ask me to part from you;
 We were joined with blood; we cannot separate;
 I stood together with you at the goat-trough,
 I saw your spear aimed, I saw killing;
 I will stand to see it again.
GRONW: And why not?
 You came to me across his corpse,
 He will take you back like Helen of old
 Across my corpse. Go, Captain,
 Take your men and escape. Tonight you can see
 The little waves of Meloch and Tryweryn
 And the smoke rising from Llanfor, and I a boy . . .
 Farewell, do not delay.
CAPTAIN: I will leave two horses for you in the courtyard.
 (The Captain and the soldiers go out. The sound of the horses leaving the courtyard. Then silence.)

BLODEUWEDD:	They have gone, Gronw.
GRONW:	While your castle turns into a prison.
BLODEUWEDD:	No one is left here but the two of us.
GRONW:	It will not last long. Before long we will have company.
BLODEUWEDD:	O if only Rhagnell would come back!
GRONW:	I would not be surprised If she came with Gwydion.
BLODEUWEDD:	I am frightened; She has never been deceitful, She was our passion's messenger, remember?
GRONW:	Remember? I remember too much. There is no pain Like the pain of failing to forget in a nightmare of living.
BLODEUWEDD:	Why must we stay here? Why must we, Gronw?
GRONW:	There is no "must" for you. "Must" is my fate.
BLODEUWEDD:	You have no weapons either. Shall I fetch you A sword and shield? Are you unwilling to fight?
GRONW:	It is not my turn to strike.
BLODEUWEDD:	Will you get down on your knees in his presence? He cannot forgive. I know my Llew.
GRONW:	I am able to dispense with his forgiveness Just to taste the tang of his spear.
BLODEUWEDD:	You want to be killed?
GRONW:	How long it has taken you to see my purpose.
BLODEUWEDD:	What are you seeking by seeking your death?
GRONW:	An hour of freedom again.
BLODEUWEDD:	I cannot understand you; The horses are still waiting at the gate And freedom in the stirrup. Why not go?
GRONW:	Freedom is here, here together with you.
BLODEUWEDD:	Your "together with you" is like wine to my heart; I was frightened a while ago, Gronw; I see now — Your freedom is to die in each other's arms, And to close life's marriage-feast defying providence.
GRONW:	No, it is not in your arms, my freedom, But in looking at you, my life's end at hand, And cherishing your sister death more than you.

BLODEUWEDD: Tossing me away? Blaming me for a spell
That turned you into a murderer? Pleading with Llew
That you did what you did because of a woman's guile?
Is this how you gain freedom, my handsome Gronw?
GRONW: No need for you to fear. It is not your death
That would give me life. Brief minutes, woman,
Are all I have, and then your husband comes,
And then death comes to me. I make that choice,
And in that choosing is my total freedom.
BLODEUWEDD: Your freedom now is to escape from me?
GRONW: I can only escape from you through death,
The poison of your kisses is in my blood,
What shall I live for? To taste for a lifetime
What I have tasted already, the sating of the flesh
And a hundred futile satings' shame and sadness?
Your lust is a grave with no tomorrow; no baby
Will laugh upon your breast; our castle has no cradle;
But at night there has been the noise of a wretch, mind gone,
Moaning upon firm breasts within the darkness,
Corroding defilement and an owl's mocking laughter.
I strayed from human paths to follow the fire
And magic pipes of the marsh, and I sank in it,
Embracing a star, a bat upon my lips;
Today a bolt came to strike me and I woke;
I see Penllyn, I see my boyhood there,
And I see myself now, ah disgusting, and you —
I prefer your husband's sword to your kiss.
(Two soldiers rush in and seize Gronw; Llew and Gwydion are with them; then two other soldiers carry in a cloth-covered bier.)
SOLDIERS: They are both here . . .
Hold him now . . . He is caught . . .

(They tie Gronw's hands behind his back.)

GWYDION: We stroll through an open gate as if to a feast
And the young couple are waiting to welcome us.

LLEW: Where are your soldiers, traitor?

GRONW: All dispersed.
I alone struck you. There is no need
To search for others or take vengeance on any but me.

LLEW: Is this a plot? . . . Search the castle thoroughly.

(Two soldiers leave.)

GWYDION: And here is the handsome heir, Gronw Hir's son,
No family now, bound, no spear in his hand.

GRONW: My lord, there is no need for your men to bind me;
I have waited for your will; I stand here for your vengeance
As freely as you yourself stood on the goat-trough.

GWYDION: That is true, nephew. I knew his father
And the castle beside the lake. Untie his bonds
We must honour a lord set for death's punishment.

(The soldiers untie the ropes.)

LLEW: That is a cord of flax upon his arms;
I was bound by the rope of a woman's falsehood.

GRONW: What do you want, my lord?

LLEW: Your life.

GRONW: You have a right to that. You will have it gladly.

LLEW: You were a full year preparing my death,
For a whole year you had possession of my bed,
My castle, my lordship, and that half-demon there
Who was called my wife. But that is not
Why I want your blood, but because you heard
And laughed at my soul's deepest secret,
Mirth at a young man's pain, and made sport of
A husband's confession, adoring the fruit of his love.
Your betrayal cut you off from the family of men;
By that act, you gave your youth to the swine;
The brand of the forest is on you; you cannot live.

GRONW: My brother, how do you wish to kill me?

LLEW: Uncle Gwydion, how shall I deal with him?

GWYDION: We shall go together this afternoon, we three,
              To the river Cynfael and the goat-trough;
              Then he can stand where you stood
                  At the front of the goat-trough, and you where he was,
              And he will be struck in the back just as he struck.
              And there will be no laughter there, and no physician.
GRONW: And no tears, but a welcome for punishment. I will come back
              To the family of men through the one common gate
              That gathers all to its shade. Thank you, my lord.
LLEW: Take him and guard him until afternoon.
              (Exeunt Gronw and the soldiers. Silence.)
BLODEUWEDD: Uncle sorcerer, you have travelled far today.
              Can I make dinner for you both?
GWYDION: Your husband has already tasted your poison.
BLODEUWEDD: You need not fear. Rhagnell will soon come back.
              She can prepare the food and I will serve.
GWYDION: Rhagnell has come back already. There she is.
              (Blodeuwedd lifts the covering from the bier.)
BLODEUWEDD: This is your work? You have drowned her?
GWYDION: We found her body in the river near the goat-trough.
BLODEUWEDD: She was a sister to me, the only one
              Who sought no profit from me, but stretched a hand
              And forgave, and went to her grave without a word of blame.
              Do you wish to drown me also now?
GWYDION: I told you that we did not drown her.
BLODEUWEDD: She was always quiet, and she died without a sound.
GWYDION: Like a wise maid, she forestalled her punishment.
BLODEUWEDD: What have I done to deserve punishment?
GWYDION: Poison, betrayal, murder, charming a man to his death,
              Trifles like these are not to everyone's liking.
BLODEUWEDD: Am I the first wife ever to be unfaithful?
GWYDION: I do not say that. There are many of your kind.

BLODEUWEDD: You are a sorcerer, Gwydion, steeped in lore,
Powerful and presuming to bind nature
And toy with the powers that are in the rocks.
Why? To feed an appetite. You had a nephew;
You cherished him more than your own children —
Understandable! — adopted him as heir
And thought of how to raise him sometime to Math's throne
As king of Gwynedd and a father of kings.
But certain terms were fixed upon his life,
Fetters of a fate that set him apart;
There are men like this, men who have been exiled
And cut off from the human race. But you,
The sorcerer-scientist, master of creation's secrets,
It went hard with you that your heir was burdened with shame;
You wished to bend the elements to satisfy your pride,
Challenging fate, cast a spell on the waves of the sea,
Conjure the spirit of the forest into a flesh and blood woman.
And so I was bound to serve like a slave-girl
To give your nephew children, establish his line,
And lull him at night to forget his unlucky birth.
Answer me, Gwydion, was that not the plan?

GWYDION: Is it tyranny to expect a wife to give her husband a son?

BLODEUWEDD: Thank you, sorcerer. Arianrhod's son was fated
Never to gain a wife among the daughters of men
Nor to breed a son. He would not yield to his fate,
Neither he nor you; I was captured as a weapon,
A tool in your hands to cheat destiny.
Am I the one who was unnatural? I begged him,
This youth not made to be cherished, to look at me
And desire me once for myself alone;
But he wanted to croon to his son
And he told his last story to the heir of his hope;
He would not come from his dreams' tomorrow

	Into the empty today of my heart.
LLEW:	It is true, Gwydion. She has been wronged. She does not deserve to die like the other one.
GWYDION:	You can say that? I find it incredible.
BLODEUWEDD:	Gronw has chosen to die. Rhagnell has died. What good is it to me if life is further prolonged?
LLEW:	I came here bitter to take vengeance on you; I see now you were always to be pitied.
BLODEUWEDD:	You defied your fate. I too was defiant; We both have writhed against necessity.
LLEW:	There is necessity in every human marriage.
BLODEUWEDD:	Necessity and craving are my passion's nature.
LLEW:	And that is the reason I forgive you. A rational soul cannot love like you.
BLODEUWEDD:	One could. I gave you him as an heir.
LLEW:	And he has chosen death to escape you.
BLODEUWEDD:	And out of jealousy you wish to kill him Because he could cherish and kindle passion. What will you do without me, poor man, Who will never gain a wife among the daughters of men?
LLEW:	Accept my fate, make my nest within frustration.
BLODEUWEDD:	I hear your mother's laughter and her glee.
LLEW:	You do not hear her sobbing in the night.
BLODEUWEDD:	Your hearth will be cold, your bed cold forever.
LLEW:	Everyone is an exile; a cold hearth is the world; I will be one with men in their bitterness.
BLODEUWEDD:	Your fate is to exist without knowledge of passion.
LLEW:	All the passion I had I gave to you.
BLODEUWEDD:	A scant scrap of your bountiful self-pity.
LLEW:	I put my life into your hands. You betrayed it.
BLODEUWEDD:	So that I could gain life. Take your revenge.
LLEW:	I cannot take revenge. I let you go free.
BLODEUWEDD:	My lord is so gracious. I can go free To my family, to my kinsmen, to my sweetheart. And where will you go now? To your mother?
LLEW:	I will go to the goat-trough this afternoon, Myself and Gwydion and Gronw Pebr of Penllyn; Will you come there to laugh as you did before?

BLODEUWEDD: Gladly, sweet. I did not know you could jest so well;
Until then I will go to the woods. Farewell.
And good day to you, uncle.
GWYDION: Yes, niece,
But listen before you go. The woods contain
A bird who is terrifying like you,
And like you is fond of the night, and its shriek
Is a portent of death like your laughter,
And all other birds are its enemies;
Your stay among men has been ill-fated;
Enter the darkness to join the owls,
The rites of the moon and the hollow tree. This moment,
As you cross the threshold and cringe from the sun
Your harsh laughter will change to an owl's screech,
And by day you will never dare show your face.
BLODEUWEDD: I will fly to Arianhod's castle. Your sister will give
An extraordinary welcome to her daughter-in-law.
(She goes out laughing. Then the laughter ends and the screech of an owl is heard)

CURTAIN

THE KING OF ENGLAND'S DAUGHTER

Siwan
(1954)

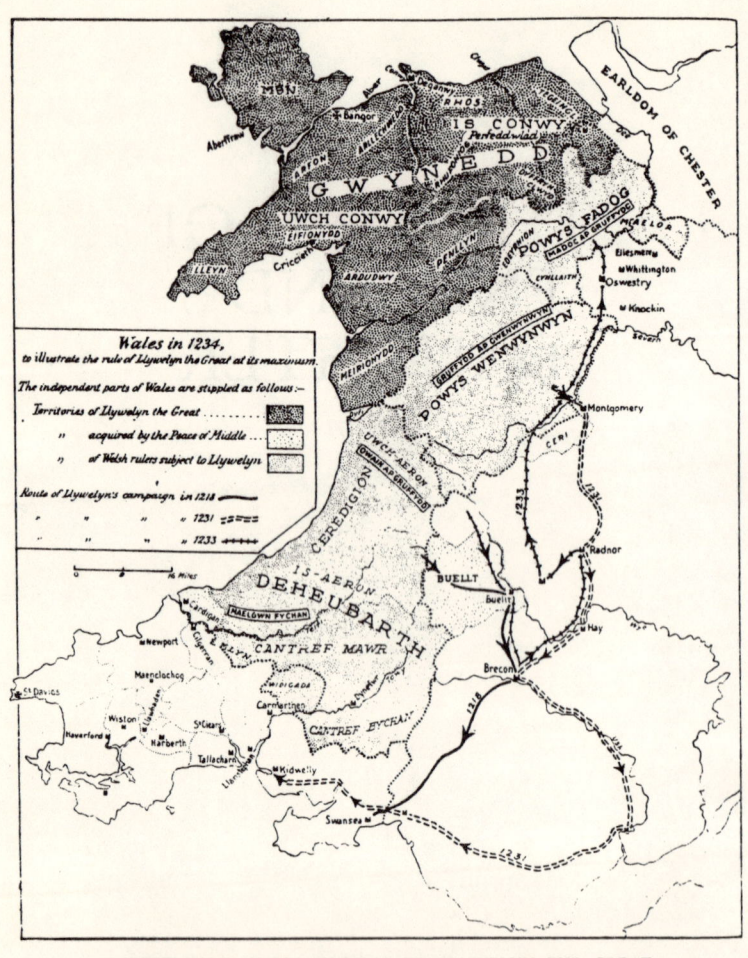

INDEPENDENT WALES, SUBJECT TO LLYWELYN THE GREAT.

Reproduced by kind permission of
William Rees, *An Historical Atlas of Wales* (London, 1959).

When his play *Siwan* was first published in 1954, Saunders Lewis called it "a creative poem, not the work of an historian". The play nevertheless assumes as well as provides some knowledge of Wales in the earlier thirteenth century. The following information is given as an aid to the reader and a basis for programme notes.

The history of medieval Wales before its conquest is marked by the frequent attempts of the rulers of Gwynedd, in the north, to unite the other regions under their leadership. When Llywelyn ap Iorwerth, later known as Llywelyn the Great, achieved power in Gwynedd in 1199 A.D., the rulers of the virtually independent regions of Wales acknowledged the overlordship of the king of England. Llywelyn's purpose during the forty years of his reign was to gain the allegiance of these rulers in north, central, and south Wales; to create alliances with the Anglo-Norman lords of the border districts, "the March"; to be recognized by the English crown as in effect though not in title "Prince of Wales"; and to pass on the rule of a unified Wales to his one legitimate son Dafydd rather than to divide it among his heirs (as had been Welsh custom). In all of this he was remarkably successful, by a skillful combination of military campaigns and diplomacy. He married Joan ("Siwan" in Welsh), the illegitimate daughter of King John and the sister of Henry III, and he arranged marriages for his son Dafydd and four of his daughters to members of the ruling houses of the March. Llywelyn's court at Aberffraw, on the island of Anglesey, remained the centre of Welsh power throughout his long reign. Much of the unity he had achieved was lost when his illegitimate son Gruffydd claimed a share in Gwynedd during Dafydd's short reign, but it was regained by the first Llywelyn's grandson, Llywelyn ap Gruffydd, who was acclaimed "Prince of Wales" at a council of Welsh rulers in 1258, and whose death at English hands in 1282 meant the end of Welsh independence.

The Welsh *Chronicle of the Princes* states that in 1230 A.D. "young Gwilym Brewys [Guillaume de Braose], Lord of Brecknock, was hanged by the Lord Llywelyn in Gwynedd, after being taken in

Llywelyn's chamber with Llywelyn's wife, the King of England's daughter." This event forms the basis for Saunders Lewis' *Siwan*, and I have used the final phrase in the chronicle as the suggested title for productions using this translation. Mr Lewis commented that "the hanging of Gwilym Brewys was a shock to the whole feudal nobility of Europe. Not his execution, but the hanging, the punishment given to common thieves. Why? Why? It was from reflecting on this that this play developed."

CHARACTERS

Llywelyn ap Iorwerth (Llywelyn the Great), Prince of Gwynedd, 57 years old
Siwan, his wife, the King of England's daughter, 35 years old
Gwilym Brewys, Lord of Brecon, 25 years old
Alis, handmaid to Siwan, 20 years old
Soldiers, etc.

TIME

Act I   The First of May, 1230, after midnight
Act II May 3, 1230, 6 a.m.
Act III The First of May, 1231

SCENE

Llywelyn's court in Arfon, above the Menai strait, across from the island of Anglesey.

ACT I

The bedchamber of Llywelyn and Siwan. Candlelight. Siwan is taking off her formal gown with the help of her chambermaid, Alis. Outside are the sounds of a harp and small fiddle playing an old French dance, and the sound of young people laughing, some of them calling "Good night!" The music continues through the opening of the act.

ALIS:	There, the silver gown is off at last, *madame*;
	I will put it in the chest at once.
SIWAN:	And this crown as well, Alis . . .
	What time of night is it?
ALIS:	I heard the soldiers on the walls
	Calling midnight some time ago, I'm sure.
SIWAN:	Have you been waiting long?
ALIS:	Not long. When I came in from the lawn
	I turned the hourglass over, and see, the sand
	Is not yet past the halfway point.
	So I must have been here for half an hour.
	Wasn't the dancing on the lawn delightful?
	The lords of France were pleased.
	I heard one of them marvelling to find
	The dances of Aquitane on a mead in Arfon.
	They know nothing of your court, *madame*.
SIWAN:	The music is ending. The last lanterns are disappearing.
ALIS:	The great lantern remains.
SIWAN:	The moon? Yes.
	Its light comes piercing through these windows.
	There's hardly a need for candles.
ALIS:	In the light of the moon and the lanterns the galliard
	Was like a dance of enchantment and faerie magic.

	I've never seen anything lovelier than the phantoms and shadows of phantoms

I've never seen anything lovelier than the phantoms
    and shadows of phantoms
Gracefully moving to an unseen harp.
How was it that you did not dance, *madame*?

SIWAN: With that heavy crown on my head?
And that silver gown like a pavilion around me?
Even for French dancing one must be more supple
    than that.
My task tonight was to preside from the chair
And take the Prince's place in his absence.
This was a dance to celebrate the pact with Brecon's
    Frenchmen.

ALIS: There's no once can dance the French carols like
    you.
When it's time for the wedding dance, you will be
    asked to lead it.
You have at the marriages of all your children.

SIWAN: Gwladus, Margaret, Helen, and now Dafydd,
Dafydd to enrich whose realm I have given my life.
Yes, I will dance at Dafydd's wedding.

ALIS: May I loosen your hair and comb it now
And arrange it so that you can sleep?

SIWAN: Do that, Alis. The crown has been a burden on my
    head;
Besides, I like to have my hair combed.
I'll sit on the stool . . . There you are.

ALIS: *(Singing softly while combing)*
Le roi Marc était corracié
Vers Tristram, son neveu, irié;
De sa terre le congédia
Pour la reine qu'il aima . . .

SIWAN: I don't like your song tonight.

ALIS: Marie de France, *madame*.
It was from you I learned it.

SIWAN: And I from my mother.
She stayed with my grandfather in Gloucester
And sang her songs of Aesop and taught them to
    my mother.

ALIS:	And your mother heard her sing the tale of Tristan?
SIWAN:	Yes, and taught it to me. It is too sad a story for tonight.
ALIS:	Marie sings like a country girl, Our feelings, our fears and our yearning, Not like the learned bards who are clever and cold.
SIWAN:	But she learned from the learned bards.
ALIS:	She was as good a bard as Prydydd y Moch And her French is easier for a Welshwoman than the Prydydd's Welsh. When will a Welsh bard come to sing simply to girls?
SIWAN:	He will come when a tavern comes to Wales.
ALIS:	I've heard there is a tavern in Glamorgan . . . *(Singing again)* *En sa contrée en est allé,* *En Sud Galles où il fut né . . .*
SIWAN:	Leave Tristan and Iseult alone. Hurry up and finish with my hair.
ALIS:	Was Tristan a Frenchman, *madame*? He was born in South Wales, *En Sud Galles où il fut né.*
SIWAN:	Is Caerleon Wales or France?
ALIS:	When I look at Gwilym Brewys, So young and lively and full of laughter, I see him as another Tristan . . . *(Siwan boxes her ears)* *Madame* . . . What have I said wrong?
SIWAN:	Have you finished with my hair, girl?
ALIS:	Look in the bronze mirror, *madame*, Two plaits like Iseult herself. My lip is bleeding where your ring struck me.
SIWAN:	Its taste will be a bridle for your tongue. Did you give the wine I left to my door-keepers?
ALIS:	Didn't you see them as you returned?
SIWAN:	Both were sleeping nicely, One on either side of the door.
ALIS:	The door-keepers sleeping?

|||Shall I wake them?
SIWAN: | What need? Let them sleep,
| Since tomorrow's the First of May.
ALIS: | It's already the First of May.
| The lads and the lasses there on the hills
| Will dance around the maypole hand in hand
| And then disappear in couples
| Before bringing it home with the dawn.
| Country youngsters have their pleasures too, *madame*.
SIWAN: | Have you been one of the youngsters, Alis?
ALIS: | *(With a low reminiscent laugh)*
| Of course, at fifteen . . .
| Were you ever beneath the maypole?
SIWAN: | *(Suddenly bitter)*
| I was daughter to a king. At fifteen
| Mother to a prince and envoy of Aberffraw.
| I gave my womb to politics like every king's daughter.
ALIS: | How still the trees are; I don't hear the sound of the sea.
| Menai must be at the ebb.
| I would fling off a queen's burden
| On a Mayday eve like this.
SIWAN: | You don't know what you're saying.
| Take your candle and go to your room and your bed.
| I've no wish to sleep just yet.
| I will knock on the floor if I need you.
ALIS: | Good night and God be with you, *madame*.
SIWAN: | God and Mary keep you, good night.
| *(Siwan softly sings "Pour la reine qu'il amia". Alis exits. A knocking at the door, twice. Siwan opens it to Gwilym Brewys.)*
GWILYM: | My lady?
SIWAN: | Gwilym? Come in. *(She closes the door softly.)*
GWILYM: | You have kept your maid a long while, with me waiting.

SIWAN:	Today, at dawn, my brother sails for France.
GWILYM:	Henry? King of England?
	Well, what is that to me?
SIWAN:	You are still a boy.
GWILYM:	I am twenty-five years old and the father of four girls.
SIWAN:	I never see you as anything but a strapping lad who was wounded
	And taken as a prisoner of war and brought here to be tended,
	My perpetual boy.
GWILYM:	What about your brother the King,
	What matter if he goes to France?
SIWAN:	Only that that is why
	I have kept the maid rather long.
GWILYM:	To hamper my coming here?
SIWAN:	This is Llywelyn's bed. There is danger here.
	If Ednyfed Fychan or one of the Council saw you
	Slip away from the lawn and the dance, and told the Prince,
	Who knows, with the King in France, what harm it would do?
GWILYM:	Don't be afraid. No one saw me coming.
	Your door-keepers were asleep.
	You drugged their wine?
SIWAN:	A precaution, when you are so reckless.
GWILYM:	You needn't worry; I've long been one of the family.
	My widowed stepmother is the Prince's daughter and yours,
	You gave a daughter to my cousin in marriage.
	And now I give my daughter to your son.
	We must be related somehow?
SIWAN:	A pity the girl isn't older.
GWILYM:	Isabella? She is eight.
	Her sister was three when my father married her.
SIWAN:	Gwladus Ddu was a second wife. Your father had an heir.

| | If Isabella is wed this year there are still six years
Before she comes here to Dafydd;
There can be no heir to Aberffraw for a year after that.
That is a long time; a danger to Aberffraw's policy,
With the Prince already fifty-seven years old.
I would like to hold my son's son, Llywelyn's heir,
Above the baptismal font as a crown on my life's work. |
|----------|---|
| GWILYM: | Dafydd has mistresses. |
| SIWAN: | Where are your brains, Gwilym?
The happy Welsh age of children of the grove and the bush
Is over for the Prince's family. Why did I take such pains
To have the Pope acknowledge my own legitimacy
Except to establish Aberffraw's line from father to son,
Like Julius Caesar's, a flawless royal succession? |
GWILYM:	Gruffydd has sons.
SIWAN:	Gruffydd? The bastard, the concubine's son?
GWILYM:	The Welshman's son.
SIWAN:	*Touchée.* I know.
Twenty years ago I gave him as a hostage to my father
Trusting in my father's way with hostages.
I was disappointed. Yes, Gruffydd has sons;
That's why there's need for haste to give Dafydd a son.
GWILYM:	Don't you want this marriage?
SIWAN:	The Prince is the one to decide. Of the two reasons for the marriage,
Which is more important, to safeguard the borders of the realm
Or to secure a son as heir? This is a long-lived family;
If Dafydd has his father's life-span both ends will be gained.

	Llywelyn has taught me one lesson in politics,
	That patience is a condition of success ... Patience is hard for me.
GWILYM:	And what lessons have you taught him?
SIWAN:	You are married and have a nestful of daughters; you know
	There is nothing for a wife to teach her husband.
GWILYM:	Don't talk nonsense. What ordinary lady-wife
	Is a land's chief minister and envoy
	And walks the halls of kings like Helen of Troy?
SIWAN:	That is my escape. I had, along with my blood,
	My father's fierce wild energy. To hold my life on course,
	I flung myself into a man's work, into my husband's work.
GWILYM:	Have you heard what they say of you in the courts of Glamorgan and the March?
	That Gwynedd is a French domain and that this is your doing;
	Llywelyn is the first of his line to give his sons and daughters
	Not to Welsh wives or husbands, but all to noble houses of France.
	You have fashioned your Prince into one of us,
	And taught the Welsh how to marry.
SIWAN:	Don't frighten me tonight, Gwilym. You might as well say
	That Llywelyn loves me like you. For it is love that changes men.
GWILYM:	You are the first successful politician I've found who's intelligent, Siwan.
SIWAN:	There's no room for love's disorder in ruling a family and a land.
	Only once have I let my heart interfere with policy.
GWILYM:	And when was that, you sensible woman?
SIWAN:	When I arranged the marriage
	Of Aberffraw's heir and the daughter of wild Gwilym Brewys.

GWILYM:	The best thing you have ever done, noble Princess.
SIWAN:	The worst, if Dafydd does not have a son.
GWILYM:	You astonish me, Siwan.
SIWAN:	How is that, lad?
GWILYM:	You know why I came here?
SIWAN:	To arrange the marriage of your daughter and my son Dafydd.
GWILYM:	You know why I want the marriage?
SIWAN:	Why did your father want it? And your cousin in Gower?
	Builth, Elfael, Brecon, — is there a need to explain?
	Wedding Aberffraw's heir strengthens your house.
GWILYM:	Siwan, those are things said while bargaining in the Council.
	That's not my reason.
SIWAN:	Don't talk foolishly. You have no son as yet.
	Four daughters cannot keep Brecon intact.
	May I arrange marriages for the three who are left?
GWILYM:	I haven't come to your room tonight to talk politics.
SIWAN:	With you, talking politics is a safeguard for me.
GWILYM:	What safeguard do you need?
SIWAN:	To believe that my life is worth living.
GWILYM:	Are you afraid of the truth?
SIWAN:	Not afraid of the truth, but afraid, perhaps, to hear it;
	A thing can be tamed in the mind that is wild in the ear.
GWILYM:	I'm not frightening you, Siwan?
SIWAN:	Not at all; but there are things in myself
	You awaken that frighten me.
GWILYM:	The things that make life sweet.
SIWAN:	The things that make living bitter,
	Things that were mute, and that I hid from my own sight,
	Because I had no share in them, because I was an exile
	Here, and my sole value is my value for the growth of a land.

GWILYM:	So you know why I came to arrange the marriage?
SIWAN:	Do I? . . . No, I don't know . . . That can never be.
	Business and pleasure are separate things, Gwilym.
GWILYM:	Pleasure? The love I have given you is no pleasure.
SIWAN:	No light-winged flattery from you tonight.
	Is it because I'm too old that your love is a torment?
GWILYM:	I haven't come here to be mocked and ridiculed.
SIWAN:	Remember that I'm ten years older than you
	And the mother of four children? That is not mockery.
	My son Dafydd is not much younger than you.
GWILYM:	I was ten years old at my father's wedding in Hereford
	When I saw you, Princess, the very first time,
	Leading Gwladus Ddu, the baby-bride,
	As the crowd in the church strewed roses before you.
	I did not speak a word to you, I could not,
	My heart was in my throat and I was breathless.
	But I snatched a rose that your feet had trod
	And that was my pillow that evening,
	I wet its leaves with a boy's joyful kisses.
	I did not see you again until I came here
	A prisoner, wounded, and my ransom a land's ransom.
	My wound was light but I had a fever,
	And I tossed and turned on a fretful bed;
	And then you came in the midst of your maidens
	Walking slowly as at the wedding in Hereford
	To the foot of my bed, and bent,
	And put your lips upon mine.
	I fainted —
SIWAN:	You gave us all a fright.
GWILYM:	You know my wound was not the reason.
SIWAN:	How
	Could I have known it that night?
GWILYM:	That kiss was a doom like Iseult's kiss —
SIWAN:	Quiet, Gwilym, don't speak of unhappy things.
	Tristan and Iseult's tale is like a nightmare tonight.

GWILYM: The weeks of my recovery were no nightmare,
The riding beside you and wine amid the rocks of Gwynedd,
The after-dinner singing. The halls of Arfon
Were like part of the bliss of Toulouse in those days.
And then the dancing and the revelling at night,
And the way your kiss turned from a kiss of courtesy
To a foretaste and a promise of this tonight.

SIWAN: Remember Hywel ab Owain's songs?

GWILYM: I couldn't believe it!
An uncle of Llywelyn, that shrewd man of business,
Singing of a white fort on Menai's bank
Songs as silken as the Arabs'?
That was the night you first put a flame in your kiss.

SIWAN: The next day Llywelyn returned with your ransom payment.

GWILYM: He has a gift for returning at the wrong time.

SIWAN: We had only a wary week after that.

GWILYM: That is why I came back. The pact with the Prince
And this marriage, I arranged them for the sake
Of returning to you, possessing you, and tonight.
Siwan, you knew that.

SIWAN: No, I did not know. I did not dare to know.
I did not believe that you would give
Your castle in Builth and your daughter, great pledges —

GWILYM: I would give all my realm for this night with you.

SIWAN: All your wealth? Like Francis the Grey Friar?
Love is as insanely prodigal as sanctity
And both despise the world.

GWILYM: Do you follow the fashion of this new saint?

SIWAN: He preached to the wolves. That is the saint for you.

GWILYM: I have heard that when Francis
Was young, he gambled and was reckless;
I like men who can put their lives at stake

	And lose as cheerfully as the cuckoo. If Francis was such a man,
	Well, that is the saint for me.
SIWAN:	I will pray to him for you
	That his intercession may protect you from misfortune.
GWILYM:	But not from tonight. Fortune is an angel tonight;
	I will turn to Francis' prayers when I lose Fortune and you.
SIWAN:	You love danger too much; your reckless bravado
	Forces me, a hardened woman, to fear for you.
GWILYM:	I must be taken, Siwan, as I am; since childhood
	Hunting, gambling, and warfare have been my element;
	That's the way to squeeze the grapes of life and sense
	Fully the tang of the taste on the palate.
SIWAN:	Am I a bunch of grapes?
GWILYM:	Upon my oath, I don't know.
	The taste of things is important to me. The taste of you
	Is a lust and a constant craving that's a torment and sweet.
SIWAN:	Have you spoken of this to any at my brother's court?
GWILYM:	To whom could I speak?
SIWAN:	Or told someone it was I
	Who suggested Easter for arranging the terms of the marriage?
GWILYM:	Yes, perhaps; I said that
	To the Chancellor, Hubert, who asked the terms for the Council.
	What does it matter tonight, Siwan?
SIWAN:	What does it matter?
	Only that Hubert de Burgh is a venomous snake
	And my husband Llywelyn was with him two days ago.
	He will come back with Hubert's poison in his ears.

GWILYM:	Though Llywelyn might fear the worst, he is a statesman,
	He would save his anger till he had the castle in Builth, —
	I know the Prince.
SIWAN:	That is more than I could say, I believe,
	Who am married to him for a quarter of a century;
	A prince and a statesman can have feelings like a man.
GWILYM:	Never mind him. You've given tonight to me.
SIWAN:	I give tonight to you. Tonight, I give
	My very self to you, — in my husband's bed.
GWILYM:	You know that I worship you?
SIWAN:	A middle-aged married woman?
GWILYM:	A ruler and princess of a royal line,
	Age has not left its mark on your brow or your body.
	The sum of the years cannot touch my adoration.
SIWAN:	Not tonight, if there were only tonight.
	I give myself to you for tonight, Gwilym Brewys.
GWILYM:	Tonight will be enough tonight, and tonight to me is forever.
	Can you not love me, Siwan?
SIWAN:	I do not know yet. Yielding is enough tonight.
	Tomorrow, who knows? Perhaps I shall love you tomorrow
	When tonight is only a remembrance and a yearning.
GWILYM:	You yourself summoned me to you tonight.
	It was you put the poppy in the door-keepers' wine.
SIWAN:	I myself, alone. Tonight is my gift to you.
GWILYM:	And why, Siwan? Why, my generous giver?
SIWAN:	Because you remember the taste of things
	And taste is gone so soon;
	Because you laugh at danger
	And life at stake is so fragile;
	Because your joy is in my power
	And to give you joy is sweet.
	Because it is now the First of May.

(Far off the voices of two watchmen are heard calling:
>TWO O'CLOCK
>TWO O'CLOCK
>ALL'S WELL)

GWILYM: Listen to the watchmen, Siwan;
It is May-Day and all is well.

SIWAN: May-Day and all is well.

GWILYM: The bed invites us, Siwan.

SIWAN: Come to the window first
To breathe the softness of the air.
Tonight I give my five senses the freedom to do as they please.
See the moon in its waning
Setting over the forest of Anglesey
And Menai in the shadow, out of sight and mute;
I cannot hear its wave upon the strand.

(For a moment the sound of horses' hooves is heard in the distance.)

GWILYM: Do you hear a sound in the distance like horses galloping?

SIWAN: Wild colts, perhaps; they are found in the foothills.

GWILYM: No, the sound of horseshoes.

SIWAN: I don't hear anything.

GWILYM: Nor I now. It has stopped. Strange too,
I've a perfect ear for the sound of horses.

SIWAN: There's a cloud hiding the moon. Look to the right, far off,
There's the Plough and the North Star
And great Arcturus behind them;
I would like to hear them singing
As they spin on the glass overhead.
They say that little children hear them as they sleep
And smile at the tune in their slumber.

GWILYM: Isn't that the planet Mars, over there?
I was born under Mars.

SIWAN: "War-mongering, crimson-hued,
Never at peace, Mars and his brood."

GWILYM: "Force of Nature, folks' unease,
No comfort for his enemies."

(They laugh. The barking of a large dog is heard some distance from them.)

SIWAN: What was that?

GWILYM: Some dog over there by the gate. One of the watchmen's dogs.

SIWAN: Gelert?

GWILYM: Which is Gelert?

SIWAN: Llywelyn's hound. I recognize his voice.

GWILYM: That cannot be. He took the dog with him
To hunt the King's forest on his way home.
There's a dog for you! I saw him bound after a stag
From cliff to cliff with a leap no stallion would dare.

SIWAN: It is odd. I am sure I know Gelert's bark.

GWILYM: It is easy to make a mistake at night;
Staring into the gloom of night raises bogies.
In the French countryside on May-Day Eve
Witches fly through the air and the dogs bark.
Why are there no witches here in Wales?
I have never heard of a Welshwoman
On trial in a bishop's court for making love with a devil.

SIWAN: In Wales the men are more attractive, especially the children of Mars.

GWILYM: Siwan, my generous giver, these candles are going out
And the royal bed is inviting;
May I have my joy before the darkness covers us?

SIWAN: Hush! Listen!

GWILYM: I hear nothing.

SIWAN: Over there by the gate, the noise of people stirring
As if someone were arriving.

GWILYM: Imagination, imagination. There is noise in every royal fortress
Every hour of the night. You have thin ears tonight.

SIWAN: I wonder? I hope — Hush! Again!
(A heavy door is heard opening and closing fifty yards away from them.)

GWILYM:	That is the fortress door opening and closing. The soldiers
	Are changing their watch. Don't be uneasy.
SIWAN:	The soldiers don't open the door in changing the guard.
	Something is going on. I hear people running.
	Look! There are torches moving and the courtyard's full of shadows.
GWILYM:	I wonder? I wonder?
	(The noise of clashing weapons and soldiers' footsteps is heard.)
SIWAN:	What is it, Gwilym?
GWILYM:	*(Finally convinced)*
	Soldiers in arms surrounding this tower.
	You are right, Siwan, something is going on.
	I will take a candle to see if your door-guards are stirring.
SIWAN:	Have you a sword, Gwilym?
GWILYM:	No sword, no knife, nothing. I will just be a moment
	Going downstairs to the door.
	(Gwilym stands at the door, the candle above his head; then the sound of a trumpet announces the Prince.)
SIWAN:	He is here! ... Gwilym, Llywelyn is in the fortress.
GWILYM:	And twenty armed soldiers around the door below.
	This is a plot. We have been betrayed, Siwan;
	The trap was closed while we gazed at the stars,
	And the deed shows a general's hand.
SIWAN:	Can you escape between the bars of the window?
GWILYM:	The gap is too narrow. Where is your maid's chamber?
SIWAN:	Below, on the right side of the door.
GWILYM:	Is there anything above?
SIWAN:	The tower platform. The door is locked.
GWILYM:	*(Laughing quietly)*
	There is nothing to be done. The Prince must be welcomed to his chamber.

	And judging by the hubbub he won't be long.
	Our welcome must be simple, with no fuss.
	(The tread of soldiers is heard nearby and the sound of shields and spears.)
SIWAN:	Come to my arms on the bed. I give myself to you, my dear.
	(The door is struck open and Llywelyn rushes in, armed soldiers with him.)
LLYWELYN:	Rip open the curtains ... Here he is ...
	Hold him. Bind him hand and foot.
GWILYM:	There's no need. Don't lose your head. I have no dagger, no weapon.
LLYWELYN:	Bind him ... Set him on his feet ...
	Gwilym Brewys, I captured you once in battle;
	As a prisoner of war I gave you a courteous welcome,
	The freedom of my court, a pact, treatment of your wounds.
	This is the repayment, making Aberffraw's Princess a whore,
	And myself a cuckold to make sport for the courts of France.
GWILUM:	Shouting whore and cuckold is the rhetoric of wounded pride.
	I love a married Princess like hundreds of lords in Christendom,
	Something that is part of an earl's life, like a tournament.
	You have caught me in your bed. Very well. I will recompense your dishonour,
	I will recompense your wife's fidelity.
	Besides giving the castle in Builth and my daughter to your son.
LLYWELYN:	*(Laughing bitterly)*
	Pay recompense for dishonour? The lords of France are amusing fellows.
	Your freedom after honourable fighting cost
	A third of your wealth, Gwilym Brewys.

	All your wealth cannot pay recompense for tonight.
	I will take your castle in Builth. I will take your life as well.
GWILYM:	*(Quietly)*
	That is more than you dare. Your anger, my Lord,
	Makes you lose your good sense. Every baron in France,
	In England, in the March, would rise against your tyranny
	And leave your realm in ruins.
LLYWELYN:	Though the Pope and all
	Christianity rose against me, I will have your life.
GWILYM:	Is that how it is? Oho! Oho!
	So it is not your pride or princely dignity that is hurt:
	Only the rage of jealousy! Siwan, my Lady,
	What other princess in all of Europe
	Has a husband —
LLYWELYN:	Shut his mouth, soldiers,
	Tie his mouth with a cloth.
	(Gwilym laughs while they choke off his voice. There is no malice in his laughter.)
SIWAN:	My lord, may I ask you a question?
LLYWELYN:	You?
SIWAN:	Two days ago you saw my brother the King on his way to France?
LLYWELYN:	Your brother the King? What about him?
SIWAN:	Was it later, from Hubert de Burgh, that you heard of this?
LLYWELYN:	And if it was from Hubert, does it lessen your whorishness?
SIWAN:	Montgomery is in his possession, and Erging,
	And he holds Cardigan and Carmarthen.
LLYWELYN:	Is this the moment to recite Hubert's assets?
SIWAN:	You know the Earl of Gloucester's health is bad;
	If he, Gilbert, should die, Glamorgan will fall
	Completely into Hubert's hands. He will have
	A realm in Wales no smaller than Gwynedd.

LLYWELYN:	*Ma dame*, this is not a council,
	But treason, filth, defilement of my bed and my wife.
SIWAN:	Brewys has no heir.
	He alone stands betwen Hubert and Gwynedd,
	He alone between Hubert and your son Dafydd.
LLYWELYN:	He alone. There he is, your chosen one.
	No, you shall not have your chosen.
SIWAN:	If Gwilym is killed Brewys' lands will be divided;
	The way will be open for Hubert to attack Gwynedd.
	Did you rush home so that Hubert's plans could succeed?
LLYWELYN:	*Ma dame*, your concern for me tonight is clear.
SIWAN:	It is not easy to strip oneself of a quarter-century's discipline.
LLYWELYN:	It was easy to strip off your clothes and fling your purity to the swine.
SIWAN:	I have wronged you. I confess it. But I am arguing now
	For your realm and Dafydd's realm.
LLYWELYN:	Do you want to prove it was for their sake
	That you took this scoundrel to bed with you?
SIWAN:	I want you to think carefully. I do not see
	That putting horns on your head is a reason for pulling your teeth.
LLYWELYN:	Adultery is not enough for you. You have lost shame as well.
SIWAN:	I am a Frenchwoman and a King's daughter,
	With no taste for the Welsh passion for morality.
	Go preach to the concubine in Dolwyddelau.
LLYWELYN:	A Frenchman for a Frenchwoman, eh? That's your suggestion?
SIWAN:	I am defending your life's labour against a moment's madness.
	Gwilym Brewys' life is important to your realm.
LLYWELYN:	Gwilym Brewys' life is precious to you.
SIWAN:	Well, and if it is?

LLYWELYN: If it is, he dies.
SIWAN: And your realm, and your son Dafydd's inheritance?
LLYWELYN: To hell with the realm and with you. I have lost my wife;
And you shall lose your lover.
SIWAN: You dare not kill him.
LLYWELYN: *(To the soldiers)*
Take him to the cell.
SIWAN: My brother the King will come from France. You dare not.
LLYWELYN: He shall hang lke a highway robber.
SIWAN: Gwilym!
LLYWELYN: He shall hang.
(Siwan runs towards Gwilym. Llywelyn strikes her in the face and she falls to the floor.)
LLYWELYN: I never thought that I would strike you . . . Take him away . . .
Take her too and lock her in the tower room.

CURTAIN

ACT II

Siwan's prison, a tower room. Outside, below, the sound of hammering and sawing wood and striking posts with a mallet at times during the first part of the act. The act begins with the opening and closing of the cell door, and Alis approaches Siwan's bed.

ALIS:	*Madame*, have you awakened?
SIWAN:	No. I have not slept.
ALIS:	Not at all? Not for two whole nights, *madame*?
SIWAN:	I'm not accustomed to an iron chain around my ankle
	Binding me with a shackle to a wall and a bed.
	The chain is heavy, Alis, the Welsh fashion in bracelets;
	Hold it, feel its weight, the weight of a prince's wrath.
	(She drags the chain along the floor)
ALIS:	The weight of his disappointment, *madame*;
	His disappointment is heavier than his anger.
	Does it hurt much?
SIWAN:	It hurts my pride so much
	That I cannot feel the pain in my leg.
	I myself before this have ordered people imprisoned
	Without ever imagining the experience,
	The disgrace in having one's feet in shackles.
ALIS:	The Prince said that the chain is just for today.
SIWAN:	Why today and not after today?
	Can today change my existence?
ALIS:	I can make your existence easier. I have wine here.
SIWAN:	He was the one who sent you here?

ALIS:	To wait on you and do your errands;
	I may come and go; the porter has his instructions.
SIWAN:	The porter is a mute. All day yesterday
	I saw no one but this mute at the door.
ALIS:	A mute porter cannot spread stories.
SIWAN:	Nor carry messages from prison.
	That is why a mute was chosen.
	Then why may I have a maid to do errands now?
	Is there to be some change in my life?
ALIS:	Will you have a cup of white wine?
	(She pours the wine into a cup.)
SIWAN:	The wine is tart; good, I am thirsty . . .
	Is today the third of May?
ALIS:	Yes, the third, *madame*.
SIWAN:	Two days, two nights, and the muteness of the cell,
	How distant is the First of May.
	Have you ever slept alone in a room, Alis?
ALIS:	No, *madame*, I am no princess.
	I have only slept on the floor as one among many.
SIWAN:	A prison's solitude is different. It surprises me,
	The hermit's world, where the tongue is worthless.
ALIS:	You have never been talkative, *madame*.
SIWAN:	No, I know. To have nothing to talk about
	In the midst of merriment has often been a burden to me.
	It is not my own silence that's a burden here,
	But the mute walls, the mute porter, and the uncertainty.
	In daylight yesterday I could hear for hours
	My own heart pulsing in my ear with worry.
	What time is it, Alis?
ALIS:	Six in the morning.
SIWAN:	The sixth hour since midnight. Add twenty-four to that,
	Another twenty-four, and I've been here about sixty hours.
	I heard a teacher, once, a follower of Augustine,
	Say there is no time in eternity. I hope that is true.

|||Staring into the eyes of time is the beginning of madness.
|||There is time for everything in time; there is no safety,
|||But a threat like that hammering that began before dawn.
ALIS: | You haven't slept, *madame*, not for three days,
|||Or touched the food that was sent to you.
|||It's no wonder your nerves are distraught.
SIWAN: | Why have you been sent to me this morning?
ALIS: | To wait on you and be at your command.
SIWAN: | It was the Prince himself who summoned you?
ALIS: | Yes, *madame*, he himself.
|||Otherwise the porter would not have opened the door.
SIWAN: | There is some mystery here. Did he speak to you
|||Of coming and going and doing errands for me?
|||And may you carry a message from prison to prison?
ALIS: | I don't know about that. He didn't speak of that.
SIWAN: | I have no other errand . . .
|||What is that endless carpentry on the lawn?
ALIS: | Some military work. I don't rightly know.
SIWAN: | Didn't you see as you crossed the courtyard to come here?
ALIS: | I noticed nothing. I had orders to hurry.
|||Does the wine warm you, *madame*?
SIWAN: | Go to the window and look. This chain
|||Fastens me to the wall like a bear to a post.
|||And you are no bitch to bait me, my girl.
|||If my father, the King, had seen a chain on my ankle . . .
|||What are they building? Go to the window and tell me.
ALIS: | There are soldiers there, *madame*.
SIWAN: | I know there are soldiers there. You said that already.
|||Soldiers have never before built a wooden contraption

	On the lawn of the court. Gwynedd cannot go to war
	Over this. That's no work of warfare down there.
	Tell me what it is that they're building?
ALIS:	There's no way to see clearly through the bars of the window.
SIWAN:	A lie, girl. You can see everything easily.
	I have often looked through the window myself before today.
	Answer me, what is happening?
ALIS:	O don't, *madame*, don't ask me again.
	I beg you on my knees, give me permission to leave.
SIWAN:	Poor thing, what is wrong with you? Don't tremble and cry.
	Tell me quietly what they are making on the lawn.
ALIS:	A gallows, *madame*, a gallows.
SIWAN:	A gallows? *(She laughs incredulously.)*
	Fair enough, Llywelyn. Is that my punishment?
	Your anger is greater than I had supposed . . .
	Dear Alis, don't cry about that.
ALIS:	Not for you, *madame*, not for you —
SIWAN:	What?
ALIS:	A gallows for Gwilym Brewys.
	(Siwan falls to the floor in a faint, dragging the chain in her fall.)
ALIS:	Porter! Porter!
	(Alis runs to the door and pounds on it wildly.)
	Hurry, open the door, open it!
	(The door opens and the mute porter comes in.)
	The Princess has collapsed, she has fainted,
	Come and help me to lift her . . .
	Here she is . . . Take her feet . . .
	(They place Siwan on the bed.)
	Go fetch a bowl of water. Hurry . . .
	A bowl of water, do you understand?
	(The mute exits slowly.)
	The sweat on her forehead! I have only the bed-linen . . .

Here's the water . . .
(The mute enters with water and a cloth.)
Wet the cloth and put it on her forehead . . .
That's it . . . She's coming to . . . *madame, madame* . . .
Open your mouth and take a sip of wine.
There now. She's coming to her senses,
Her eyes have stopped rolling in her head . . .
You gave us a fright, my Lady . . .
Get out, porter,
She's motioning for you to leave.
(The porter exits, closing the door and locking it; the noise of the work outside has stopped.)
He has gone. There's no one but me, *madame*.

SIWAN: I'm all right now . . . I didn't fall on the bed?
ALIS: No, straight to the floor.
The porter and I lifted you onto the bed.
SIWAN: I am ashamed.
ALIS: It's no wonder,
With no sleep or food for three days, and the shock.
SIWAN: Was I long before I came to?
ALIS: No, a few moments. Why?
SIWAN: The sound of the hammering and the mallet has stopped.
Has anything happened yet?
ALIS: Nothing at all, *madame*.
It fell silent this minute, as you came to your senses.
SIWAN: Good. I would not want to escape that way.
Have the workmen finished? Go and see.
ALIS: They're gathering their gear and sitting on the lawn.
SIWAN: It's always a long wait, they say, once the job is finished.
How was he condemned? By the judge's court? Or the Prince himself?
ALIS: The whole thing was over by noon-time yesterday.
All morning the court was buzzing like the door of a beehive

	With whispering, stories, murmuring, and nothing certain,
	And the Prince's servants turning pale and trembling at every summons,
	Only the whites of their eyes to be seen.
	Bishop Cadwgan was with the Prince at dawn;
	We heard he suspected it was through some sorcery
	That the young Earl came to you.
SIWAN:	Poor compassionate bishop,
	His purpose was to calm the Prince's rage.
ALIS:	And console him, too, perhaps.
SIWAN:	And who knows
	That it was not sorcery? There is a power
	Like supernatural power in the shock of love;
	People are lucky that love's a rare thing in this world.
ALIS:	Your head is bleeding where you struck the wall.
SIWAN:	The bleeding will reduce my fever. What happened then?
ALIS:	Then the Council was summoned.
SIWAN:	Was my son there?
ALIS:	No, he was sent to Cardigan yesterday.
SIWAN:	Good. How were things managed?
ALIS:	Some people say
	That Ednyfed Fychan pleaded for his life to be spared
	For fear of affronting the King and the lords of the march.
	When that failed, he argued in favour of beheading,
	An execution proper for a baron. The Prince would not listen;
	He wanted a robber's punishment, to hang him by daylight in public;
	Arguing with him was like reasoning with a peal of thunder.
	Ednyfed Fychan himself was pale when he left the Council
	Like someone who has barely escaped a bolt of lightning.

SIWAN:	When was the verdict announced?
ALIS:	Yesterday afternoon, *madame*. The hanging is this morning
	Before mass. It was announced from the door of Bangor Cathedral
	Yesterday, before market closing in the churchyard.
	The crowd has been waiting two hours outside the gate.
SIWAN:	He knows?
ALIS:	Yes.
SIWAN:	When was he told?
ALIS:	Bishop Cadwgan was with him last night for an hour.
	He is with him now.
SIWAN:	Is there any news of him? Have you heard how he is?
ALIS:	No one may approach his prison or the men
	Who attend him. The knights who came here with him
	Are also locked up till today. But last night, *madame*,
	After the bishop left him, I went secretly
	Past the tower cellar. I heard him singing.
SIWAN:	What did he sing, Alis?
ALIS:	Marie de France —
	Le roi Marc etait corracié
	Vers Tristran, son neveu –
SIWAN:	Have you ever seen a hanging?
ALIS:	Yes, of course, *madame*, many times,
	Bandits and thieves. Haven't you?
SIWAN:	No, never, strange to say.
ALIS:	When it's thieves, the whole thing is a show
	That draws more of a crowd than a fairground fool.
	And if the man is afraid, there's sport as good as a jester's,
	Pushing him to the top of the ladder and putting the rope round his neck
	And tying the hood on his face. Then, of course,

	One must say a Hail Mary quietly while the priest
	Hears his confession or makes the sign of the cross;
	After that comes the shouting, as on a saint's feast-day.
	I once saw a pirate at Borth
	Make jokes on the ladder and drink a toast to the crowd
	And as he was hung pretend to dance with his feet.
SIWAN:	Are they a long time dying?
ALIS:	Some long, some short.
	Some give a jerk with their feet after hanging for half an hour;
	It depends on how the ladder is tossed and how
	The rope is knotted.
SIWAN:	Who tosses the ladder?
ALIS:	The soldiers or the executioners underneath it.
	I've heard it said, if the rope is tied firmly
	And one gives a sudden leap, a man can kill himself
	In a second. I've never seen that;
	The girl who saw it said that the leap
	Thrusts his tongue through his mouth past his nostrils,
	And before the jerk is over and his feet are quiet
	His backbone has snapped. The thieves prefer
	To fall cautiously into the knot; then they stay
	Fairly long before the face is squeezed black.
SIWAN:	Holy Mary, help him to leap like Gelert.
	(The sound of military trumpet and drum)
	Go to the window, Alis, and tell me what's happening.
ALIS:	O *madame*, he is your lover.
	I never thought I would see a nobleman hang
	Who came here to marry his daughter to the heir.
	And he is so young, spilling merriment
	Around him like a fountain bubbling with laughter;
	He has often kissed me on the lip and tickled my chin.
	The court of Gwynedd will never be the same after today.

(The crowd is heard rushing and shouting –
             DEATH TO THE FRENCHMAN
             TO THE GALLOWS WITH BREWYS)

SIWAN: Go to the window, girl, or I'll split this chain.
ALIS: You cannot bear it, *madame*.
SIWAN: I said I was ashamed of my weakness before.
I won't fall in a faint or scream or shed a tear.
It will only be a few minutes. I will go through this with him.
I will kneel on the bed near the crucifix.
Stand where you can see best.
(She drags the chain onto the bed.)
ALIS: There's a crowd shouting.
The soldiers are now in a square round the gallows
And the mob is milling about them.
THE CROWD: Death to him . . .
To the gallows with Brewys . . .
Down with France . . .
ALIS: How disgusting a crowd is. The sight of the Welsh down there
Is like the picture of Doomsday in Bangor Cathedral
And the swarm of the damned and the devils.
Isn't the human face a horrible thing?
If we really stand in a crowd when Doomsday comes,
Poor wretches, Hell will be our proper residence.
(A low drumming, to suggest a military funeral.)
Here come the choir and the canons of Bangor from the hall
Chanting the litanies in their procession.
We can hear them now as they pass the tower.
CHOIR: *Omnes sancti Pontifices et Confessores*
                                                    orate pro eo.
Sancte Augustine   *ora pro eo.*
Sancte Benedicte   *ora pro eo.*
Sancte Francisce   *ora pro eo.*
SIWAN: *(Low)*
Saint Francis, pray for him that his hands are left free

	So that he can leap.
	Saint Francis who loved the wolves, pray for my wolf.
THE CROWD:	Brewys to the gallows . . .
	The gallows for Brewys . . .
CHOIR:	*Omnes Sancti et Sanctae Dei*
	Intercedite pro eo.
THE CROWD:	Death to him . . .
	The devil take him . . . To hell with him . . .
CHOIR:	*Propitius esto, parce ei, Domine.*
ALIS:	The crowd is a crush as far as the walls and the gate;
	It's hard for the soldiers to hold them back, even with their spears.
	(Drum and trumpet call)
	Here come the court officials, Ednyfed Fychan in the lead.
SIWAN:	Is *he* there?
ALIS:	The Prince? There's no chair for him on the lawn;
	So he must not be coming. No, he's not with them.
	He can see all that happens from his chamber.
	Ednyfed is in charge; I see him setting the ranks in order.
	The crowd is quieter now with his eyes upon them . . .
	(A drum again and a trumpet call)
	Here come the Prince's household guards. The prisoner will soon be here;
	The guardsmen are forming a line on each side of the walk
	From the court to the lawn to guard the way to the gallows,
	Each man with his shield and spear. There's a yard between each of them,
	Two yards between the two lines . . .
SIWAN:	*(Low)*
	Mary, I dare not pray. I don't know how to pray.
	Make a bargain with a sinner, O Mother of sinners:
	I will welcome a lifetime in prison if he may leap.

ALIS:	Here are the six French knights who came with Gwilym Brewys:
	They are walking two by two in black shirts
	Without armour or weapons. It's certain that they
	Will go back with the corpse to bury it in Brecon.
THE CROWD:	Down with France . . .
	To the gallows with France . . .
	Wales forever . . .
	(Drum and trumpet call)
ALIS:	Now, now, here is the Bishop of Bangor with his prayer book,
	And right behind him, here he is, *madame*, Gwilym Brewys.
SIWAN:	How does he look?
ALIS:	He's in shirt and trousers; barefoot; a rope round his neck,
	And the captain of the guard holds the end of the rope in his hand.
	His arms are free, and his hands.
SIWAN:	His arms and hands free! He can leap, leap!
ALIS:	They are passing here now, he and the Captain and the Bishop
	Between the two files of soldiers.
SIWAN:	Is he sad?
ALIS:	Seeing them you'd think that the Captain was going to be hanged
	And Gwilym Brewys was courteously leading him to the gallows.
THE CROWD:	Hooray! . . . . Hooray! . . . Hooray!
	To the gallows with him . . . Wales forever . . .
	Wales forever . . .
ALIS:	The crowd has seen him. They are now on the lawn.
	It is close to the final minutes.
	(The drum beats slowly and low)
SIWAN:	*(Low)*
	Saints of God who dare to pray, pray for him.
ALIS:	He is shaking hands with Ednyfed Fychan and the Council

	One by one like a lord receiving them at his table;
	He has a word for each one, they're all laughing...
	Now he is on his knees before the Bishop
	And Cadwgan makes the sign of the cross above his head.
	The crowd is silent, stunned,
	And the Council is standing there paralysed.
	No one moves but Gwilym. He is testing the ladder;
	Now he's feeling the rope, he puts it round his neck,
	He bows and says farewell; he's climbing like a ship's captain
	To the top of the ladder, straightens up —
SIWAN:	*(Low)*
	Now and at the hour of his death, amen.
ALIS:	The executioners aren't moving to twist the ladder.
	(Gwilym's shout is heard clearly)
GWILYM:	Siwan!
	(A moment's pause, then a scream of terror from Alis)
SIWAN:	*(Quietly)* Is that the end?
ALIS:	But the leap that he made, the leap.
	The rope on the gallows whipped like a fishing-rod,
	The ladder was tossed into the midst of the Council...
	Now his body is quivering like a tree-trunk twisted by a crane;
	It's growing still now, still and limp.
	(A low drumming and a final trumpet)
	The crowd is pouring out. For them
	The show is over and was disappointing. What do they know, what do they care
	About a widow in Brecon, or a woman prisoner here
	Faltering in anguish? Pain is leprosy,
	A lair of darkness in daylight, a mystery;
	No one has ever felt compassion for pain.
	Go, people, and dance to the harp. The fiddlers and minstrels
	Are already on the tump playing Wales forever.

	(The music of harp and fiddle is heard outside – playing "Men of Harlech"(?) It fades away.)
ALIS:	*Madame*, is someone coming? I hear soldiers' footsteps.
	(The door is opened. Soldiers. Then Llywelyn.)
LLYWELYN:	Remove the chain and shackle from her foot. The danger is over now.
	Leave, all of you . . .
	(They leave and close the door.)
	It is all over now . . .
	I wouldn't dare, eh? I wouldn't dare?
SIWAN:	From the depths of the hell in my soul, my curse upon you, Llywelyn.

CURTAIN

ACT III

The morning of May-Day, 1231. Llywelyn is in his bed-chamber. A knocking at the door.

LLYWELYN:	Come in.
	(Alis enters.)
ALIS:	My lord, my mistress is making ready;
	She will be here in a moment.
LLYWELYN:	I sent my son to escort her. Is he with her?
ALIS:	He is with her now;
	She sent me to tell you.
	She didn't see him on his wedding-day, sir.
LLYWELYN:	She hasn't seen him for a year;
	I know that, girl . . . Is your mistress well?
ALIS:	As well as she can be, sir, after a year of prison.
LLYWELYN:	Seclusion, not prison. She's had everything but her freedom:
	Two maids to attend her and a close to walk in.
ALIS:	Yes, sir, she's had everything but her freedom.
LLYWELYN:	What is on your mind? Tell me what you are thinking.
ALIS:	An order, sir?
LLYWELYN:	An order.
ALIS:	Lord Dafydd was married. His mother was not at the wedding
	And did not lead the bridal dance. She was left with her memories.
LLYWELYN:	My son was married, as arranged, to Gwilym Brewys' daughter;
	It would be hard for his mother to dance in the widow's house.

ALIS:	A bridal dance is a ceremony.
LLYWELYN:	For a royal family, life is a ceremony.
ALIS:	She has changed, my lord.
LLYWELYN:	Everyone changes; even memories change;
	Anger and vengeance change.
	How has your mistress changed? What change have you seen?
ALIS:	She hasn't beaten me for a whole year!
LLYWELYN:	Have you deserved to be beaten?
ALIS:	*(Laughing)* I don't know, sir.
	Beating maids is a matter of custom, not desert.
LLYWELYN:	And she has stopped the custom?
ALIS:	My lord, she was young in spirit before her imprisonment.
LLYWELYN:	That is not what's on your mind. Say what you're thinking, girl.
ALIS:	I have said what I dare, sir.
LLYWELYN:	It was the hanging of Gwilym Brewys that aged her,
	Her liveliness went with Gwilym to the hangman's noose.
	That is what you think.
ALIS:	That is what I fear, sir. You asked me.
LLYWELYN:	I must ask someone.
	A year without a beating makes you bold.
ALIS:	I am no serf's daughter, sir. My father was a free man.
LLYWELYN:	You are married too, I believe.
ALIS:	I am a widow for the last three years, my lord.
LLYWELYN:	Forgive me. He was one of my household guard;
	He was killed at Baldwin's Castle; a courageous boy.
ALIS:	I saw him once before I became his wife;
	Then, after a fortnight together, the war came;
	He left, and I never saw him again.
	By now it is all like a young girl's dream.
LLYWELYN:	But a dream, not a nightmare.
	He was killed while attacking the castle wall.
	Do you remember saying goodbye to him?

ALIS: At daybreak.
I gave him a sup of warm milk from the goat
And had a milky kiss amid the soldiers' laughter.
A fortnight, and all was over. We were beginning to know each other.

LLYWELYN: Every husband and wife are beginning to know each other,
Whether it's a fortnight or twenty years.
You are not without courage yourself.

ALIS: I, sir?

LLYWELYN: You did not stop living.

ALIS: Did I have any choice?

LLYWELYN: No one who is brave and intelligent
Has not at some time been tempted to stop living.
Life is a terrible gift for everyone.

ALIS: Even for a prince?

LLYWELYN: Isn't the prince a human being, girl?

ALIS: Will you tell that to the princess, sir?

LLYWELYN: Does she doubt it?

ALIS: It would help her to hear it.
Warfare and making allies and all the business of ruling
Is a hedge around the prince: his greatness sets him apart.
But for us women, yes for a woman who's a ruler,
A mother's instinct is the root of all love, and a woman's first-born
Is the husband to whom she is given as a girl;
Because she loses the child in him a woman strays, sir.

LLYWELYN: To be weak is to be human; that is your point?

ALIS: Gwilym Brewys was a child, sir, a little child.

LLYWELYN: And it is little children who enter the kingdom of love.
Very well, Alis, I will try to chew on your lesson.

ALIS: My Lord, I am only a servant; you made me speak.
I was taught in these royal chambers,
I revere and cherish their master and their mistress;
This widowed year has hurt the household and the house;

	The Pope's excommunication was child's play compared to our pain.
LLYWELYN:	The Pope's excommunication will soon be on us again
	If that matters.
ALIS:	So the story is true, sir, that runs through the house?
LLYWELYN:	Is there a rumour at court?
ALIS:	That you are starting a war once more with the King of England.
LLYWELYN:	That is to be settled today by your mistress;
	She is the one to choose, warfare or death to Gwynedd.
	That's why I've summoned her now from her year of prison.
	The fate of Wales is in her hands.
ALIS:	Here comes the princess, sir.
LLYWELYN:	Wait close by in the maids' chamber.
	I will need you, I hope, before long.
	(Siwan enters. Alis exits.)
SIWAN:	You sent for me, my lord. Here I am.
LLYWELYN:	Siwan!
SIWAN:	My lord?
LLYWELYN:	Siwan! *(There is no answer)*
	Siwan! It is I, Llywelyn . . . Siwan?
SIWAN:	Llywelyn?
LLYWELYN:	I need you, Siwan . . . I, Llywelyn. *(There is no answer)*
	I need you, Siwan.
SIWAN:	You need me?
	How can that be?
LLYWELYN:	Why not?
SIWAN:	I have been a prisoner for months, my lord.
LLYWELYN:	For a year this morning. I have counted the days.
SIWAN:	Is it May-Day today? I have lost count.
LLYWELYN:	It is the First of May.
SIWAN:	Must a prisoner be treated so churlishly?
LLYWELYN:	What churlishness? What are you thinking?

SIWAN:	Today, of all days . . . here to this chamber, Straight from my prison? Why have you summoned me here?
LLYWELYN:	To continue the conversation we had here last year.
SIWAN:	*(Completely calm and self-possessed as if held by an iron hand.)*
	No, no, no, never again. I cannot talk about Gwilym.
	In your mercy, lord, order me to return to my cell.
LLYWELYN:	I need you, Siwan. This is a plea, not an order.
	Neither did I choose this morning to punish you.
	A message came here from the South last night;
	That is why I summoned you. Peace to Gwilym's soul . . .
	Hubert de Burgh is the burden of my cares.
	Here, that night, you prophesied about him,
	Prophesied like Cassandra. All your words have come true.
	I must go to war once more against your brother.
SIWAN:	Go to war again? That is the Council's decision?
LLYWELYN:	The council hasn't met. I am asking your counsel first.
	I will summon the others after.
SIWAN:	And why my help?
LLYWELYN:	I have a right to your help;
	Neither adultery nor prison can erase my right.
SIWAN:	Yes, you have a right. I gave you the right.
	I cannot take back your right.
	But why are you claiming your right today?
LLYWELYN:	Today my right is the right of Gwynedd and Aberffraw's Crown;
	I call on you for help and counsel according to your oath.
SIWAN:	Not a plea, then, but an order?
LLYWELYN:	Very well, if you insist. The plea will come later.
SIWAN:	Why must you go to war at your age?
	You are almost sixty.
LLYWELYN:	A message came last night, news of William Marshal's death.

SIWAN:	May he rest in peace. I have had no reports for a year, my lord; Forgive my sluggish mind. May I know Why William Marshal's death is a reason for war?
LLYWELYN:	Last year, Gwilym Brewys' lands were placed in his charge.
SIWAN:	Gwilym Brewys, his brother-in-law . . . And now?
LLYWELYN:	Now they've been given to Hubert de Burgh.
SIWAN:	Water runs downhill. One of your friends, my lord. You did your best for him.
LLYWELYN;	Have you heard that the Earl of Gloucester is dead?
SIWAN:	May light shine on Gilbert's soul. No, I had not heard.
LLYWELYN:	He died in Brittany, during the Christmas revels.
SIWAN:	That is not surprising. And the heir is a child.
LLYWELYN:	Yes, the heir is a child, And the child has been placed in the care of Hubert de Burgh.
SIWAN:	*(Laughing)* Yes, to be sure. And what of the child's lands? What about Glamorgan?
LLYWELYN:	Hubert is to hold Glamorgan.
SIWAN:	Your friend is growing uncommonly fat.
LLYWELYN:	It has all happened as you said it would, Siwan.
SIWAN:	That doesn't bring back the dead or loosen a rope. My purpose that night was to save a life; Your temper was not so politic. Peace to Gwilym's soul, Hubert's a deep one.
LLYWELYN:	His power now stretches from Hereford to Cardigan Joining Dyfed and Gower, Brecon and Glamorgan; Brewys and Marshal and Gilbert are now one in Hubert.
SIWAN:	The crown's chief minister in England as well And all the King's strength there and in France under his thumb. Is it wise for you to risk war?
LLYWELYN:	*(Laughing curtly)* Madness, I know. But what else can I do?

	Consider the land between Tywi and Teifi today, Dinefwr and Cantre Mawr and Cantre Bychan; I cannot keep the homage of the lords of the South, The Lord Rhys' grandsons, Without showing my power to protect or punish them.
SIWAN:	Is Rhys Gryg of Dinefwr still alive?
LLYWELYN:	Alive and as wild as ever, but loyal till now. Only war can keep him that way, — Hubert is on each side of him now Like a wolf, jaws open to grasp Ystrad Tywi.
SIWAN:	If Ystrad Tywi were taken, Cardigan would be lost. Hubert's South would be a realm greater than Gwynedd: Two principalities in Wales are impossible.
LLYWELYN:	That hits the nail on the head.
SIWAN:	Where is my brother now?
LLYWELYN:	The King is in England. I must attack though I know that the power Of the Kingdom of England and the March and Hubert's South Are all united against me.
SIWAN:	All united? If they were all united one could not go to war. Since Dafydd was born it has been a rule like a law That we do not go to war or incite a war While there is peace between the King and the March.
LLYWELYN:	True, but never before Have Glamorgan and Deheubarth been a single realm. War is inevitable.
SIWAN:	Certainly, War is inevitable. But one must go to war So that winning is also inevitable; Dafydd's heritage is in the balance.
LLYWELYN:	Your work and mine is in the balance.

	The burden we've borne together in our time on this earth,
	The line of Cunedda, the crown of Aberffraw, Wales.
SIWAN:	You should have thought of that a year ago.
LLYWELYN:	I considered it fully a year ago.
SIWAN:	What do you mean?
LLYWELYN:	Here, in this room, you foretold the effect
	Of killing Gwilym Brewys. In the Council afterwards
	I reported your words. I kept nothing back.
	They were weighed and appraised. Ednyfed Fychan believed them.
	The Bishop of Bangor believed them. And I believed them.
	Knowing that the crown of Aberffraw and the realm of Gwynedd
	Were at terrible risk, I hanged Gwilym Brewys.
SIWAN:	May I ask why?
LLYWELYN:	It is right for you to know why. Soon, at the right moment.
	Policy first, my lady; back to the old discipline.
SIWAN:	What is simmering, then, in England and the March? Any sign of a crack?
LLYWELYN:	Our hope rests in that. The earls and the bishops Who went to the crusade are returning.
SIWAN:	Peter, bishop of Winchester, is he returning as well?
LLYWELYN:	He has reached France. He will be in England before the end of summer.
SIWAN:	Hubert's mortal enemy. The court and the March will be at loggerheads.
	Can you put off the war till he comes?
LLYWELYN:	No, worse luck, not and keep Rhys Gryg's loyalty.
	If he and his nephews see me delay, they'll go over like mice to Hubert.
	I must launch an attack before summer.
SIWAN:	Would the beginning of June be right?
LLYWELYN:	It would be right in Powys. What of Dyffryn Tywi?

SIWAN: *(Slowly)*
Loose Rhys Gryg now to loot the wealth of Brewys
And promise you will join him soon.
At the same time send an envoy to complain of your wrong to the King
And pretend a peaceful grievance to delay his army a month.
Then the crusaders will come to see Hubert at Hereford;
And you may strike in Montgomery and burn your way down to Gwent;
The March will rise like wolves for the blood of de Burgh, —
Glamorgan and the South have always been their stamping ground;
There's a good chance you'll end the summer in Cardigan
With Hubert's realm only a memory.

LLYWELYN: *(After weighing it)*
Your counsel is shrewd and sound;
Your counsel is in the tradition of Gwynedd's policy;
Winning Cardigan back would conclude my wars like an amen . . .
I will take your counsel, my lady, on one condition.

SIWAN: Does your condition concern me?

LLYWELYN: I will take it if you return today to my bed and my table . . .
(Pause)

SIWAN: Does this mean forgiveness?

LLYWELYN: Will you accept forgiveness from me?

SIWAN: To forgive is to conquer. I have not forgiven you.

LLYWELYN: For killing Gwilym Brewys?

SIWAN: I knew that Gwilym Brewys' life would be short.
Killing him was human; I could forgive that easily.
But because he loved me,
And because I yielded to his love,
You gave him the death of a knave and a highway robber

	And opened your lawn to the jeering of Arfon's churls;
	You hanged him — to show your contempt
	And to spit on our love before the world.
LLYWELYN:	He died handsomely. His death was worthy of your love.
SIWAN:	He put your Council to shame,
	Your mob of serfs was silenced;
	No thanks to you for that.
LLYWELYN:	Has it crossed your mind, Siwan,
	That I might love you like Gwilym Brewys?
SIWAN:	*You* love me? What do you mean?
LLYWELYN:	Is the gap between us as wide as that?
SIWAN:	My lord, I was married to you when I was ten years old
	And you, a prince, were more than thirty.
	Four years later I came like a rabbit to your bed:
	I was your wife and your bed-mate for twenty years;
	I gave you an heir, I gave you daughters,
	I governed your household, I was an interpreter
	To plead and save you from my father's rage, to reconcile you with my brother;
	I wore myself out in the tasks of a bishop and envoy,
	Travelling in your service; I built a realm with you:
	Once, before I grew old, a young man came, played a harp to my barren heart, —
	You hanged him like a herring on a string.
LLYWELYN:	That is true. I am sorry for that today.
	He had to die. He did not have to be hanged.
SIWAN:	Then why? Why? I cannot live with you,
	I can never share the same sheets without understanding why.
LLYWELYN:	You cannot understand why. I don't exist for you.
SIWAN:	You exist as a nightmare exists since that morning.
LLYWELYN:	I know that. Your Gwilym was closer to me:
	He saw me as a person.
	I had to shut his mouth before he betrayed me in front of you.

SIWAN: Will you tell me what Gwilym saw?
In the name of twenty years of sleeping together
I have a right to know.
LLYWELYN: To tell you is to bare my breast to the arrows of mockery.
SIWAN: A year of prison in solitude drives away mockery.
LLYWELYN: Our marriage was politics, my lady,
And between us the gap of a quarter of a century.
Well, that is the custom, the foundation for countries'
Treaties and concord, bearing together, building together.
But four years later, when you came,
Like a young silver birch, a virgin to Snowdonia,
My heart suddenly twisted as if I had seen the Grail.
For me there was light wherever you walked,
But I smothered my bedazzlement lest it should frighten you
And when I felt you here, trembling in my arms,
I did not bruise you with clumsy kisses
Or the sweat of dreaded embraces; I kept myself tightly in check
So that you would not find me disgusting. I was gentle, courteous, formal;
And your trembling disappeared: this chamber became your home
And I a part, not too unwelcome, of the furnishings.
So I worshipped you, my flame, at a distance and mute,
And avoided trespassing with words of fondness;
But I drew you into the business of my life,
I ruled my house, my family, my realm by your counsel,
And I gave your splendid mind the room to function.
I remember the afternoon you returned from your father

                From your first embassy — my life
                Was in danger that time. You were fifteen years old
                And your son Dafydd scarcely two months. You came home,
                My life and Dafydd's principality
                Safely beneath your belt. And that night
                You embraced *me*. I had no language
                To speak my rapture; I mastered my body's trembling; —
                But after that night I was a terror to my enemies:
                I collected Cardigan and Powys and Deheubarth
                And set them in your son's crown, for him alone in Wales
                In spite of Welsh custom, in spite of the split in my house;
                I insisted he be recognized by the King of England and the Pope
                And had the Pope proclaim the flawless royalty of his line.
                I was architect of all this: it was my temple for you,
                My way of worshipping you —

SIWAN: Llywelyn, I didn't know, I didn't know.
LLYWELYN: What was the good of your knowing? The mountains of years were between us.
                I understood that too;
                I am a politician, I didn't seek the impossible,
                Your loyalty was enough.
SIWAN: In twenty years of living together you never said this before.
LLYWELYN: In twenty years of living together you never saw this.
SIWAN: So it was out of jealousy that you hanged him?
LLYWELYN: There was jealousy perhaps in killing him;
                You were the reason he was hanged.
SIWAN: I? I?
LLYWELYN: On that terrible journey,
                As I galloped day and night through Powys
                And across Is-Conwy, I knew in bitter disillusion

	That Hubert spoke the truth and that here I would find the lively lad
	On my bed, in your arms, without weapons.
	The journey was long enough to smother the yearning
	To bury a dagger in his heart; he would die like a baron after sentencing.
	So he would have died but for you.
SIWAN:	For God's sake, why?
LLYWELYN:	In your contempt for me you judged that policy possessed my soul,
	That I would barter my bed for a castle
	And let my wife be defiled for a treaty and a border.
	I answered contempt with contempt:
	I hanged him to make your warnings come true
	And to show a wife who spurned me underfoot
	There was one thing for which I would throw away Aberffraw's crown and Cunedda's Wales.
SIWAN:	Llywelyn, Llywelyn,
	Because of reckless contempt you have drawn this war upon you,
	And you almost sixty years old! Government is not a playground.
LLYWELYN:	Your contempt that night transformed
	Half a century's plans of government into dung.
SIWAN:	By the Saviour's Cross, Llywelyn,
	Contempt was not what I intended.
LLYWELYN:	The unintended word is the key to the heart.
SIWAN:	There is no key to a heart;
	There is no one on this earth who understands another;
	The husband embraces the wife and the wife responds with a kiss,
	Two planets fixed in their orbits; they never hear each other.
LLYWELYN:	Isn't that what marriage is, to bind oneself without knowing,
	To give oneself, defenceless, not knowing to whom or what chance?

	The child and the full-grown man are in the same trap;
	What is living but a game of chance?
SIWAN:	Your war is choice, not chance.
LLYWELYN:	That depends on you:
	Will you return to my bed and my table?
SIWAN:	What has that to do with your war?
LLYWELYN:	The war is inevitable. One can choose to return.
SIWAN:	I am a prisoner. It was your verdict parted us.
	Why not order me to return?
LLYWELYN:	You must return to me of your own will.
SIWAN:	And if I refuse?
LLYWELYN:	Very well. I shall go to war.
SIWAN:	And not return? The threat is unfair.
LLYWELYN:	A princess and a King's daughter? You are long familiar
	With sentencing and hearing men sentenced to death.
	It is part of our daily life.
SIWAN:	I cannot come to your bed unless I have your forgiveness.
LLYWELYN:	You know that is to be had.
SIWAN:	It is not to be had. I will not ask forgiveness
	Nor bear forgiveness from a self-righteous hypocrite . . .
	You are watching Llywelyn the Great over there in the mirror
	Forgiving his wife as the weaker vessel
	Before going into the peril that she stirred up with her sin.
	I have listened to you and learned: *I* defiled your bed;
	I hanged my lover as well, *I* gave Hubert the South,
	I endangered Dafydd's realm through this war,
	I shattered the image before which your life was a lamp,
	You martyr of marital love.
	And now before leaving for battle you will take me back to your bed

                And floor me with the grace of your forgiveness to weeping in dust and ashes,
As you, with the sun on your helm, ride splendidly off to your death.
After bearing your body home, Llywelyn, I'll fetch a painter from France
To put on the wall of the chapel on Conway's bank
The Parable of the Prodigal Wife and the God-like Husband.
(A moment of silence. Then both break out laughing.)

LLYWELYN: I am not worthy of you Siwan.

SIWAN: Every wife has heard that sometime:
That is when the husband is most dangerous.

LLYWELYN: Can you forgive me, Siwan?

SIWAN: Llywelyn the Great asking forgiveness from a whore?

LLYWELYN: A word of madness, a word of jealous rage;
My love turned to hatred and terrible malice
That night —

SIWAN: Hush, don't speak the truth.
There's no confessional here, no spiritual father,
Only a wicked wife craving supremacy.
(Both laugh again.)

LLYWELYN: Do you forgive me, Siwan?

SIWAN: For calling me that?
Dear Llywelyn, the name was completely appropriate.

LLYWELYN: But the malicious hanging? The wild pleasure in your pain?

SIWAN: Your misery is worse. Gwilym was hanged:
He leaped to his death crying out my name,
And our love had a zenith of pain and glory.
So I will remember it longer; we were spared
The hour of disillusion, the half-hearted kissing, the worn-out complaint and the surfeit.
But you must, if you forgive, live with the ashes of your idol
And remember the sleepless nightmare of the night love's flame was put out;

	Lying with me in your bed will be like sleeping alive in your grave.
	Can you stand me, Llywelyn, can you stop hating me?
LLYWELYN:	Will you come back, Siwan?
SIWAN:	Between us in bed, if I come, will be the stink of your love's defilement.
LLYWELYN:	Between us in bed, if you come, will be a corpse hanging on a rope.
SIWAN:	What will we do with them, Llywelyn?
LLYWELYN:	Stretch out our arms across them to each other
	And take them to us like souls dwelling in Purgatory;
	Marriage at its best is Purgatory, the preparation.
	I am the fire that shrivels you and kills you,
	Fire on your skin, an old man who is more of an institution
	Than a human being, the politician in bed.
	You and your memory of a lad who leaped to your kiss and his death,
	Will you come back to me, Siwan?
SIWAN:	The habit of a quarter of a century draws me back.
LLYWELYN:	The heritage of your son draws you back.
SIWAN:	The stupidity of an old man rushing off to war draws me back.
LLYWELYN:	There's a good chance I'll win the war, despite my age, with you back.
SIWAN:	Llywelyn, I will your success and your welfare.
LLYWELYN:	That is enough; you are back already.
SIWAN:	Will you take me like that, with nothing but good will?
LLYWELYN:	Good will is selfless love. Siwan, my wife,
	I shall go from my chamber into battle rejoicing
	Like a giant to run a course, the course of your war.
SIWAN:	One word, Llywelyn.
	I shall see your triumph, God willing,
	I shall see the fall of friend Hubert de Burgh,
	I shall see your realm established, and Dafydd's heritage.

	After that, my days will not be long —
LLYWELYN:	You will outlive me —
SIWAN:	No. Life is still strong in you,
	And your zest for building still vigorous.
	That is over for me.
	Will you grant me one promise now?
LLYWELYN:	Tell me your wish.
SIWAN:	My final testament. From the window of my prison room,
	Beyond the lawn of the gallows and the sand of Lafan,
	Over there across Menai, I could see Dinaethwy and Llanfaes
	And the crows rising and falling above the trees by Saint Catherine's church;
	Seeing their uncensured freedom was balm to a prisoner's heart.
	When I am dead,
	Will you take my body across in a boat and bury it
	There, in the new graveyard, and give the land
	To the Franciscans to build a house and a chapel?
LLYWELYN:	The Grey Friars? Why to Francis of all the saints?
SIWAN:	I have a debt to pay to the saint of the cord.
	He was fond of gambling and fond of a rope.
LLYWELYN:	Your wish is a wound. I had thought
	To have you with me in Aber Conwy.
SIWAN:	You appealed to the marriage vow:
	That binds me to you as far as the grave.
	And I am glad of that, I welcome that.
	But the grave breaks every bond, frees everyone:
	I would like my bones to rot there all alone.
LLYWELYN:	Very well, love,
	I will do it all according to your will, Siwan . . .
	Are you there, Alis?
	(Alis runs in)
ALIS:	My lord?
LLYWELYN:	Where is the crown of the Princess of Aberffraw?
ALIS:	In *madame*'s chest.
LLYWELYN:	Bring it here to me.

	(She opens the chest)
	This maid has been complaining about you, Siwan.
ALIS:	*Madame*, no. I have never complained.
LLYWELYN:	You haven't beaten her for a year, she says.
	She misses the sting of your hand.
ALIS:	My lord, shame on you!
LLYWELYN:	Therefore I take the burden of punishing her on myself.
	If I return victorious from this war
	I will marry you to the bravest lad in my guard
	If that is your pleasure . . . Here is the crown . . .
	My princess, I crown you
	With the diadem of Aberffraw. I give you my right hand,
	And I kiss your hand . . . To the great hall, to dine.
	This afternoon I shall summon the Council of the Realm
	And present them with Gwynedd's plans for war.
	(A trumpet sounds . . .)

CURTAIN

Appendix

THE PRONUNCIATION OF WELSH

The Welsh alphabet uses 28 letters: a, b, c, ch, d, dd, e, f, ff, g, ng, h, i, l, ll, m, n, o, p, ph, r, rh, s, t, th, u, w, y.

In general, the consonants represent the same sound-values as in English spelling, with these exceptions:

c: always the sound in 'cat', never the sound in 'cease'.

ch: as in the Scottish word 'loch'.

dd: the sound represented by the 'the' in 'breathe'; Welsh uses 'th' only for the sound in 'breath'.

f: as in 'of'.

ff: as in 'off'.

g: always the sound in 'give', never the sound in 'germ'.

ll: there is no equivalent sound in English; the usual advice is to pronounce 'tl' rapidly as if it were a single sound, or to put the tip of the tongue on the roof of the mouth and hiss.

ph: as in 'physic'.

r: the sound is always trilled.

rh: the trilled 'r' followed by aspiration.

s: always the sound in 'sea', never the sound in 'does'. 'si' is used for the sound represented in English spelling by 'sh'; English 'shop' becomes Welsh 'siop'.

Welsh letters stand always for pure vowel-sounds, never as in English spelling for diphthongs. The vowels can be long or short; a circumflex accent is sometimes used to distinguish the long vowel.

a: the vowel-sounds in 'father' and (American) 'hot'.

e: the vowel-sounds in 'pale' and 'pet'.

i: the vowel-sounds in 'green' and 'grin'. The letter is also used for the consonantal sound represented in English spelling by 'y'; English 'yard' becomes Welsh 'iard'.

o: the vowel-sounds in 'roll' and (British) 'hot'.
u: pronounced like the Welsh 'i'. Never used as in English spelling.
w: the vowel-sounds in 'tool' and 'took'. English 'fool' becomes Welsh 'ffŵl'. The letter is also used consonantally as in English, 'dwelling', 'Gwen'.
y: in most monosyllables and in final syllables pronounced like the Welsh 'i'; in other syllables it stands for the vowel sound in 'up', and this is also its sound in a few monosyllables like 'y' and 'yr'.

The following diphthongs are used in Welsh; the chief vowel comes first:
ae, ai, au: the diphthong sound in 'write'.
ei, eu, ey: 'uh-ee'.
aw: the diphthong sound in 'prowl'.
ew: the short Welsh 'e' followed by 'oo'.
iw, yw: 'ee-oo'.
wy: 'oo-ee'.
oe, oi, ou: the sound in 'oil'.

The accent in Welsh is placed, with few exceptions, on the penult: Llýwarch, Llywélyn.